Human Resources Development (HRD)
Theory and Practice

Human Resources Development (HRD)

Theory and Practice

By

Rakesh Kumar Sudan
Associate Professor and Head of Department,
University College, Kurukshetra, Haryana

and

Minakshi Sharma
Parent Educator Trainee for Child Development,
United States (US)

New Century Publications
New Delhi, India

NEW CENTURY PUBLICATIONS
4800 / 24, Bharat Ram Road,
Ansari Road, Daryaganj,
New Delhi - 110 002 (India)

Tel.: 011-2324 7798, 4358 7398, 4101 7798
E-mail: indiatax@vsnl.com • info@newcenturypublications.com
www.newcenturypublications.com

Editorial office:
LG – 7, Aakarshan Bhawan,
4754-57/23, Ansari Road, Daryaganj,
New Delhi – 110 002

Tel.: 011-4356 0919

Copyright © 2018 by the authors

All rights reserved. No part of this book may be reproduced, stored in a retrieval system, or transmitted in any form or by any means, mechanical, photocopying, recording, or otherwise without the prior written permission of the publisher.

First Published: **2018**

ISBN: **978-81-7708-463-4**

Published by New Century Publications and printed at Milan Enterprises, New Delhi.

Designs: Patch Creative Unit, New Delhi.

PRINTED IN INDIA

About the Book

Human beings are the heartbeat of an organization. They are the brain trust and think tanks of future strategies. Intangible assets, like human capital, decide the use of tangible and material resources innovatively to fulfil the objectives of any business entity.

Human resources management (HRM) relates to formulation of strategies by business entities concerning selection, training and rewarding of their personnel. Human resources development (HRD) is concerned with the development of competencies and effectiveness of people working in an organization. The design of HRD system should strengthen corporate planning, production processes, marketing strategies, and budgeting and finance.

Skills and knowledge are the driving forces of economic growth and social development for any country. Countries with higher levels of skills adjust more effectively to the challenges and opportunities in domestic and international job markets. As India moves progressively towards becoming a global knowledge economy, it must meet the rising aspirations of its youth. This can be partially achieved through focus on advancement of skills that are relevant to the emerging economic environment. The challenge pertains not only to a huge quantitative expansion of the facilities for skill training, but also to the equally important task of raising their quality.

This book provides a vivid account of the various dimensions of HRD including, *inter alia*, knowledge management, competency mapping, socialization and orientation of employees, training and development, organizational culture and organizational health. It also sets forth the policies and programmes of the Government of India to empower all individuals through improved skills and knowledge to gain access to decent employment and ensure India's competitiveness in the global market.

About the Authors

Dr. Rakesh Kumar Sudan is presently Associate Professor and Head of Department, University College, Kurukshetra, University of Kurukshetra, Haryana. He obtained M.A. (Economics), Ph.D. and LL.B. degrees from the same University in 1983, 2001 and 2007 respectively. An avid researcher, he has published a number of articles in academic journals of repute. He has attended and presented papers at various conferences and seminars.

Ms. Minakshi Sharma is presently a parent educator trainee for child development in a reputed school in the United States (US). She received her B.Com., M.Com., and M.Phil. Degrees in commerce from Kurukshetra University, Kurukshetra in 2001, 2003 and 2004 respectively. She taught commerce at DAV College, Ambala (Haryana) from 2006 to 2011. She has also attended and presented papers in UGC-recognized national seminars.

Contents

About the Book..v
About the Authors..vi
Preface...xi-xii

1. Human Resource Management (HRM) and Human Resource Development (HRD)   **1-12**
1.1 HRM: Meaning, Importance and Strategy
1.2 HRD: Meaning and Necessity

2. HRD: Importance, Emergence and Goals   **13-22**
2.1 Importance of HRD
2.2 Emergence of HRD: Background
2.3 Goals of HRD
2.4 Functions and Scope of HRD
2.5 Organizational Development
2.6 Career Development
2.7 Factors Affecting HRD
2.8 HRD Dimensions

3. Meaning and Approaches to Organizational Effectiveness   **23-31**
3.1 Organizational Effectiveness Defined
3.2 Organizational System
3.3 Approaches to Measure Organizational Effectiveness
3.4 Steer's Multi-dimensional Perspective
3.5 Time Dimensional Model
3.6 Cameron's Four-criterion Measure
3.7 Social Function Model
3.8 Robey and Sales Integrated Four Way Approach
3.9 Job Analysis

4. Knowledge Management: Dimensions and Tools   32-44
4.1 Knowledge Management Defined
4.2 Importance of Knowledge Management
4.3 Types of Knowledge
4.4 SECI Model of Knowledge Dimensions
4.5 Knowledge Management Process
4.6 Knowledge Management Barriers
4.7 Knowledge Management Tools and Techniques

5. Learning and HRD   45-55
5.1 Principles of Learning
5.2 Kolb's Model of 4-stage Cycle of Adult Learning
5.3 Theories of Learning
5.4 Learning Styles

6. Competency Mapping   56-65
6.1 Competency Defined
6.2 Classification of Competencies
6.3 Competency Mapping
6.4 Need for Competency Mapping
6.5 Process of Competency Mapping
6.6 Iceberg Model of Competency
6.7 Tools and Techniques
6.8 Management by Objectives (MBO)
6.9 Effects of Competency Mapping on Other HRD Systems

7. Socialization and Orientation of Employees   66-74
7.1 Organizational Socialization
7.2 Socialization Process
7.3 Learning in Socialization
7.4 Socialization Categories
7.5 Consequences of Socialization
7.6 Orientation of New Employees

7.7 Difference between Socialization and Orientation

8. Training and Development   75-86
8.1 Training Defined
8.2 Importance of Training and Development
8.3 HRD Process
8.4 Implementing HRD Programme
8.5 Evaluation of Training Programme
8.6 Problems in Training

9. Organizational Culture and Organizational Health   87-94
9.1 Organizational Culture Defined
9.2 Importance of Organizational Culture
9.3 Types of Organizational Cultures
9.4 Factors Determining Organizational Culture
9.5 Organizational Characteristics
9.6 Organizational Health

10. Size and Characteristics of India's Human Resources   95-108
10.1 Size and Growth of Population
10.2 Characteristics of India's Population
10.3 Demographic Dividend Hypothesis
10.4 Areas of Concern and Future Challenges

11. Institutional Set-up for HRD in India   109-124
11.1 Ministry of Human Resource Development (MHRD)
11.2 Ministry of Labour and Employment
11.3 Ministry of Skill Development and Entrepreneurship (MSDE)

12. Target Groups for Skill Development   125-141
12.1 Skill Development for Marginalized and Vulnerable Groups

12.2 Skill Development for Women Workers
12.3 Skill Development for Unorganized
   (Informal) Sector Workers

13. Recent Initiatives for Skill Development   **142-162**
13.1 National Policy for Skill Development
   and Entrepreneurship (NPSDE), 2015
13.2 National Skill Development Mission
   (NSDM)
13.3 Pradhan Mantri Kaushal Vikas Yojana
   (PMKVY)
13.4 Udaan
13.5 Skill Loan Scheme

References/Bibliography   **163-168**
Index   **169-174**

Preface

Human resources in terms of demographic trends are important, as also the development of human resources through programmes in education, health, social welfare and science and technology.

Human resources management (HRM) relates to formulation of strategies by business entities concerning selection, training and rewarding of their personnel. The subject has assumed added significance in the wake of liberalization and globalization trends sweeping across the world. In the face of intense competition unleashed by market-oriented reforms, firms are vying with each other to acquire competitive advantage to prosper in business and in many cases to survive in business. Every possible strategy is being applied to achieve the explicit and implicit objectives of the firm. HRM has emerged as an important ingredient of the policy mix to score points over the existing and potential competitors.

Human resources development (HRD) aims at improving human resources. HRD is concerned with the development of competencies and effectiveness of people working in the organization. The design of HRD system should strengthen corporate planning, production processes, marketing strategies, and budgeting and finance.

Different roles in an organization should be integrated using different mechanisms, e.g. manpower planning inputs should be available to line managers so that they can do career planning. A systematic way to monitor the progress and to identify the level of effectiveness of the system is required.

HRD managers are expected to know everything about organizational efficiency and for this they should work closely with different departmental heads in the organization. It is one of their roles to design, develop and implement the evaluation of programmes. They should assess the needs of training and development of employees, analyze the data obtained and organize further programmes for their career development.

As HRD managers are concerned about the development of

their organization, it is their prerogative to identify the threats and opportunities provided by the external environment, for instance, there is a strong need to bring advancement in technology, based on the study of external environment. Identifying the threats and opportunities helps an organization to survive and further it helps in achieving the objectives efficiently.

To manage learning is one of the most significant roles performed by a HRD manager. They should communicate the results obtained from respective decision-makers so that they can take corrective action on time. It is expected that HRD managers should clearly understand the importance of career development and when it can be brought into the system of learning.

HRD managers also act as marketing specialists. They are actively involved in the management function. Ultimately, their aim is to make and maintain favourable internal and external environmental relations for smooth conduct of the business.

Skills and knowledge are the driving forces of economic growth and social development for any country. Countries with higher levels of skills adjust more effectively to the challenges and opportunities in domestic and international job markets. As India moves progressively towards becoming a global knowledge economy, it must meet the rising aspirations of its youth. This can be partially achieved through focus on advancement of skills that are relevant to the emerging economic environment. Government of India has recently taken a number of initiatives to empower all individuals through improved skills and knowledge to gain access to decent employment and ensure India's competitiveness in the global market.

Rakesh Kumar Sudan
Minakshi Sharma

1

Human Resource Management (HRM) and Human Resource Development (HRD)

The resource base of a country consists of: (a) human resources, (b) non-renewable resources which are an endowment of nature and whose total size gets depleted with time and (c) renewable resources which can be continuously created and whose base can be expanded through human efforts.

Human resources in terms of demographic trends are important, as also the development of human resources through programmes in education, health, social welfare and science and technology.

1.1 HRM: Meaning, Importance and Strategy

According to National Institute of Personnel Management of India, "Human resources management is that part of management which is concerned with people at work and with their relationships within an organization. It seeks to bring men and women who make up an enterprise, enabling each to make their own best contribution to its success both as an individual and as a member of the working group".

HRM relates to formulation of strategies by business entities concerning selection, training and rewarding of their personnel. The subject has assumed added significance in the wake of liberalization and globalization trends sweeping across the world. In the face of intense competition unleashed by market-oriented reforms, firms are vying with each other to acquire competitive advantage to prosper in business and in many cases to survive in business. Every possible strategy is being applied to achieve the explicit and implicit objectives of the firm. HRM has emerged as an important ingredient of the policy mix to score points over the existing and potential competitors.

1.1.1 Importance of HRM:

Human resources are of critical importance for the growth of knowledge and technology, value addition and improvement of competitiveness in manufacturing through processes of continuous improvement. In fact, human resources are the only *appreciating resources* in a manufacturing system. They are the only resources that have the motivation and ability to increase their value if suitable conditions are provided, whereas all other resources—machines, building, materials and so on—depreciate in value with time. The best enterprises view their people as their prime asset and the source of their competitive advantage. Nations that have achieved sustainable competitiveness in manufacturing even when they do not have required raw materials, such as Japan and South Korea, have created systems for the continuous improvement of the capabilities of their human resources.

Human beings are the heartbeat of an organization. They are the brains trust and think tanks of future strategies. Intangible assets, like human capital, decide the use of tangible and material resources innovatively to fulfil the objectives of any business entity. Vision sharing with employees with adequate empowerment constitutes an essential element of a HRM strategy. A system of fair compensation for performance and provision of a good *work-life balance* and succession planning become important in the context of the *war for talent*, rising salaries and growing levels of attrition, particularly in developing economies like India.

HRM is a dynamic process of bringing people and organizations together so that the goals of each other are met. Since people constitute the most significant resource of any organization, management of human resources becomes critical for the success of the organization.

With the rapid changes in the business scenario in the recent past, organizations are forced to reorient themselves to meet the new challenges. Technological advances, global competition, demographic changes, information revolution and trends towards service society have changed the rules of the game significantly.

In such a scenario, organizations with similar set of resources can gain competitive advantage only through effective and efficient management of resources. HRM is no more an administrative function but a growth-oriented professional function. Human resources managers have to face a number of challenges for managing the modern knowledge-oriented organizations. In the light of these, several new issues have emerged including talent management, outsourcing, performance management, online recruitment, emotional intelligence, team management and impact of information technology and communications.

The premise that people provide organizations with an important source of sustainable competitive advantage is established. The effective management of human capital as a determinant of organizational performance is thus accepted. Competition, technology, management and the rise of the new economy, has forced organizations to look for innovative strategies to gain the competitive edge. The role of HRM in organizations has assumed significance in this context and has been evolving dramatically in recent years. The successful organizations are using human resources as a strategic partner, investing them with far-reaching transformational roles and responsibilities. This activity involves making the function of managing people the most prioritized activity in the organization and integrating all policies/programmes pertaining to human resources within the framework of a company's strategy. Indian organizations are increasingly turning to HRM techniques to face the emerging challenges posed by liberalization and globalization.

1.1.2 HRM Strategy: The HRM strategy highlights issues like talent identification, retention and engagement of employees. It has also brought out the need for a *gap analysis* and measures to fill the gaps in knowledge, talent, productivity and strategy leading to competence building and better position-person fit. A watch has to be kept on demand-supply mismatches and in-house development of multi-skilled personnel to enable companies to diversify, integrate and carry on multiple businesses. These issues call for taking new initiatives in the area of training, imparting skills and empowerment, competence mapping and career development.

Hitherto, companies in India looked at HRM as a segmented strategy. In the present context of increasing global competition, high customer expectations and emergence of novel business models, time has come when one has to revisit HRM strategy and look at it as a vital input for business. This approach involves aligning of HRM practices with business strategy and harnessing of human capital for business success. Human capital has to be deployed to secure predictable, sustainable and desirable long-term competitive advantage.

With the growing complexity of technology, customer expectations and competitive challenges, there is need for closer industry-academia interaction and more purposeful linkage of theory and practice. Companies have to accord high priority to development of people for the development of the company. This calls for aligning aspirations of the employees with the objectives of the company.

India must invest in and build its human resources capabilities to catch up with other countries that have moved ahead and thereafter sustained competitive advantages in manufacturing. Indeed the contentious debate of *labour* versus *capital* in the enterprise, could be reframed if employees are seen as assets, with value that can appreciate, rather than as labour costs. Human resources should be managed as a source of sustainable competitive advantage.

1.1.3 Chanakya's Contribution to HRM: Chanakya (also known as Kautilya or Vishnugupta) is a known guru of Ancient India for his remarkable contribution in the field of economics and political science. Let us discuss some of his contributions to the related field.

A systematic treatment of managing human resources has been provided by Kautilya in his treatise titled *Arthshastra*. In respect of labour organization, there prevailed different sectors based on logical principles, e.g. *shreni* or guild system and co-operative sector. Quantity and quality of work were the basis for providing wages and unnecessarily delays in a work or compromise with the product quality resulted in punishment. Also, to regulate employee-employer relationship, well-defined procedures were followed.

Kautilya also put light on personnel management and staffing that includes job description, qualifications needed to perform a job, process of selection, development of executives and incentive system.

The principle of division of labour was already being followed in the name of *varnashram* (caste system), e.g. *brahmins* used to earn livelihood by teaching, state management etc., *kshatris* were specialized in fighting, *vaishyas* for business, agriculture, and *shudras* for doing menial work.

Later on, these four categories of people's profession became hereditary in which the training and skills were transferred from one generation to another and as a result a number of professions such as goldsmiths, blacksmiths, charioteers, carpenters, weavers, hunters, sculptors, etc. became separate communities.

1.2 HRD: Meaning and Necessity

HRM is concerned with management of people in an organization to achieve organization's objectives whereas HRD aims at improving the human resources.

In order to achieve organizational objectives, HRM works for bringing employees and organization together whereas HRD is concerned with the development of competencies and effectiveness of people working in an organization.

The design of HRD system should be such that it strengthens other functions being carried out in the company, i.e. corporate planning, production department, marketing department, budgeting and finance.

Different roles in an organization should be integrated using different mechanisms, e.g. manpower planning inputs should be available to line managers so that they can do career planning. A systematic way to monitor the progress and to identify the level of effectiveness of the system is required.

1.2.1 Roles and Responsibilities of a HRD Manager: HRD managers should set up activities to improve employees' performance in an organization. However, their roles and responsibilities are much more and may be listed as under:

HRD managers are expected to know everything about the organizational efficiency and for this they should work closely with different departmental heads in the organization. It is one of their roles to design, develop and implement the evaluation of programmes. They should assess the needs of training and development of employees, analyze the data obtained and organize further programmes for their career development.

As HRD managers are concerned about the development of their organization, it becomes their role to identify the threats and opportunities provided by the external environment, e.g. there is a strong need to bring advancement in technology based on the study of external environment. Identifying the threats and opportunities helps an organization to survive and further it helps in achieving the objectives efficiently.

To manage learning is one of the most significant roles performed by a HRD manager. They should communicate the results obtained from respective decision-makers so that they can take corrective action on time. It is expected that HRD managers should clearly understand the importance of career development and when it can be brought into the system of learning.

HRD managers also act as marketing specialists. They are actively involved in the management function. Ultimately, their aim is to make and maintain favourable internal and external environment relations for smooth conduct of the business.

1.2.2 Globalization and HRD: Globalisation implies widening and deepening integration with the *globe*, i.e. with people and processes abroad. The trend towards the evolution of a global society is generally thought of in economic terms and in terms of the consequences of the revolution in communication technologies. There is undoubtedly much greater economic integration among the nations of the world today. Globalisation is widely seen as the most important factor that could influence economies of nations the world over in the new millennium. The rapid advancement in information technology and communications has made it not just possible but absolutely essential for economies of the world to adapt or fall by the wayside.

Globalisation has also resulted in the creation of a new business framework. More changes can be expected in the business scenario specifically in terms of openness, adaptiveness and responsiveness. The most important dimensions of economic globalisation are: (a) breaking down of national barriers; (b) international spread of trade, financial and production activities and (c) growing power of transnational corporations and international financial institutions in these processes. While economic globalisation is a very uneven process, with increased trade and investment being focused in a few countries, almost all countries are greatly affected by this process.

A major feature of globalisation is the growing concentration and monopolisation of economic resources and power by transnational corporations and by global financial firms and funds. This process has been termed transnationalisation, in which fewer and fewer transnational corporations are gaining a large and rapidly increasing proportion of world economic resources, production and market shares. Where a multinational company used to dominate the market of a single product, a big transnational company (TNC) now typically produces or trades in an increasing multitude of products, services and sectors. Through mergers and acquisitions, fewer and fewer of these TNCs now control a larger and larger share of the global market, whether in commodities, manufactures or services.

Another feature of the current globalisation process is the globalisation of national policies and policy-making mechanism. National policies (including economic, social, cultural and technological) that until recently were determined by the States and people within a country have increasingly come under the influence of international agencies and processes or by big private corporations and economic/financial players. This has led to the narrowed ability of governments and people to make choices from options in economic, social and cultural policies.

Most developing countries have seen their independent policy-making mechanism capacity eroded, and have to adopt policies influenced by other entities, which may on balance be detrimental to the countries concerned. The developed countries, where the major economic players reside, and which also control the processes and policies of international economic agencies, are better able to maintain control over their own national policies as well as determine the policies and practices of international institutions and the global system. However, it is also true that the large corporations have taken over a large part of decision-making even in the developed countries, at the expense of the power of the state or political and social leaders.

The issue that concerns developing countries is how one can ensure greater participation of the weaker economies in the global process and what needs to be done to ensure that the course of globalisation benefits more people in more countries. The uneven and unequal nature of the present globalisation is manifested in the fast growing gap between the rich and poor people of the world and between developed and developing countries; and by the large differences among nations in the distribution of gains and losses.

This imbalance leads to polarisation between countries and groups that gain, and the many countries and groups in society that lose out or are marginalised. Globalisation, polarisation, wealth concentration and marginalisation are therefore linked through the same process. In this process, investment resources, growth and modern technology are focused on a few countries, mainly in North America, Europe, Japan and a few East Asian countries. A majority of developing countries are excluded from the process, or are participating in it in marginal ways.

Although the developed world is in a dominant position and has been prepared to use this to further their control of the global economy, the developing countries have not done well in organising themselves to co-ordinate on substantial policy and negotiating positions. The developed countries, on the other hand, are well-organised within their own countries, with well-staffed departments dealing with international trade and finance, and with university academics and private and quasi-government think tanks helping to obtain information and map policies and strategies. They also have well-organised associations and lobbies associated with their corporations and financial institutions, which have great influence over the government departments.

On the positive side, globalisation has compelled developing countries to improve overall economic management, and make their economies efficient. To get a share of global capital and technology, developing countries have to upgrade their social and economic institutions through administrative, legislative and legal reforms. The quality of governance has to improve to encourage productivity and efficiency. Political stability has to be established. In this context, following lessons can be drawn from East Asian countries:

1. Developing *human capital* is a basic pre-requisite. Successful globalisation and the knowledge economy require educated, healthy and skilled people.
2. It is necessary to build up domestic savings and put them to productive use.
3. Sound economic management and macro-economic balances are necessary. Large fiscal deficit is a serious obstacle to globalisation.
4. Good governance at the national and sub-national levels builds confidence among investors.
5. Transparency has to be established in the functioning of both government and business units.
6. Free and open market economies require effective

regulatory authorities because role of government changes from control and regulation to governance and facilitation.
7. Modernised capital markets with effective regulatory authorities are necessary to impart confidence to investors by maintaining stability and regulating speculative forces.

1.2.3 World Trade Organization (WTO) and HRM:
WTO is the only international body dealing with the rules of trade between nations. The agreements have three main objectives: (a) to help trade flow as freely as possible, (b) to achieve further liberalisation gradually through negotiations and (c) to set up an impartial means of settling disputes.

In order to support more open and integrated world trading system, the WTO has taken on new responsibilities. One is the growing emphasis on transparency. Under the WTO, there are more rigorous obligations on members to notify the WTO of changes in trade policies, more frequent national trade policy reviews and new and more analytically intensive global trade monitoring reports. The aim of this work is not only to keep markets open, but, just as importantly, to share information, improve understanding and encourage dialogue.

In addition to administering the existing agreement on trade in goods (agricultural and manufactured), the WTO oversees new agreements on services and intellectual property, the trade policy review process and the strengthened dispute settlement body. Several reforms accompanied these legal and administrative changes, the most high-profile of which was the requirement for biennial ministerial conferences to guide the work of the new organization. These formal changes to the institution helped to drive important informal changes as well. One of the most striking was members' growing engagement in the day-to-day work of the WTO.

As a matter of principle and practice, members cannot be expected to implement commitments to which they have not agreed. The consensus rule also prevents the most powerful members from dominating the agenda, keeps everyone negotiating until compromises emerge, and legitimizes outcomes.

The WTO's expanding rules—as well as its binding dispute settlement system—are possible only because all members have agreed to them through the consensus principle, the procedural equivalent of the most favoured nation (MFN) rule. It ensures that the WTO operates on the basis of co-operation, not coercion, and that its rules reflect, rather than override, the interests of national governments. The recent Trade Facilitation Agreement is a striking example of how consensus agreement—and the expanding size of the WTO membership—is no impediment to innovation and reform when members have a common interest in advancing the system.

In the changed world trade scenario, the importance of HRD cannot be overemphasized. Companies will have to take appropriate steps to re-train and optimally use their human resources if they want to successfully compete with international players.

1.2.4 Total Quality Management (TQM): An important role of management is to lead an organization in its day-to-day operations as well as to maintain it as a viable entity into the future. Quality has become an important factor to succeed in this latter strategic responsibility. Total quality is a description of the culture, attitude and organization of a company that strives to provide customers with products and services that satisfy their needs. The culture requires quality in all aspects of the company's operations, with processes being done and defects being controlled.

TQM is a method by which management and employees can become involved in the continuous improvement of the production of goods and services. It is a combination of quality and management tools aimed at increasing business and reducing losses due to irrelevant practices.

Life long, learning is a process that can be done in almost every scene of life. Work place is one good platform to learn continuously. At work, one can learn how to accomplish certain tasks, how to behave in making decisions, how to treat other people within the organization, and how to cope with the everlasting changes. If a company is to develop the ability of continuous self-renewal, its real battle lies in changing individual organisation members' behaviours and actions. In the late 1980s, providing customer satisfaction in customer terms became a specific goal of business organisations. Providing high quality was recognized as a key element for success. At the end of the twentieth century, business organizations were involved in what has become a quality revolution.

Organisations everywhere are growing increasingly conscious of the competitive potential quality. Quality has become an issue because standards are now specifically defined whereas previously they were vague and unmonitored. Competition focuses not only on price but quality. In the present economic and political climate, even higher standards are demanded in the face of diminishing resources.

2

HRD: Importance, Emergence and Goals

2.1 Importance of HRD

When employees are hired in an organization, the process of investment takes place. Employees are like an investment who are expected to work hard by applying their required skills or knowledge on the task given to them, accept challenges arising due to rapidly changing business environment domestically as well as globally and due to change in technology. More and more competition is taking place in the economy due to all the above mentioned factors and need of the hour is to face these challenges by updating one's knowledge, skills, etc. not only according to current business requirements but also for survival and future growth.

Employees are provided training to upgrade their knowledge and skills as per requirement so that they can work effectively and efficiently according to the growing business needs and increasing competition. Providing training to the employees is not a one time activity but it has to be an ongoing activity depending upon the requirements.

Their productivity is expected to increase when employees are trained which is good for the organization as well as for employees. Training builds a sense of belongingness in the employees towards the company. When we talk about today's business world, employees need growth and they want themselves to be trained in different areas so that they can accept the challenges coming ahead and also it increases the level of confidence in them.

Every company wants to hire the best talent and to retain that talent. The best talents always have the lucrative offers coming from outside the company and they can leave the organization if they see that there is no growth for them in future if they keep on working in the current organization. They are concerned about their future growth too besides other benefits that they are getting. Such type of talent is required by every organization as they are confident enough to accept all types of challenges based on their updated knowledge and expertise.

Based on the above discussion, now many companies have realized the importance of having human resource development department which is separated from personnel department. The need of having human resource development department is felt by almost all the companies in the world and they have high expectation from it because bringing the concept of human resource development aims at developing human resources in every aspect, i.e. efficient problem solving abilities, upgrading skills, improving organizational health, proper application of knowledge management, increased participation etc. so that employees can contribute their best towards what is expected by an organization from them.

2.2 Emergence of HRD: Background

In the 18th century, the skilled workers who were small shopkeepers used to work themselves to produce handicraft goods etc. as per their needs. Here, we are discussing about the time when limited number of skilled workers were there who used to produce goods by themselves to fulfil their arising demand. Then later on the time came when the demand of their product increased and they felt the need to hire some workers because now they needed some assistance to fulfil the increase in demand from outside. But unfortunately none other was skilled enough to produce goods.

So, in order to solve the existing problem, the skilled workers started teaching some workers how to produce those goods and they kept teaching them until the hired workers became expert in that particular field of producing goods. They worked under their masters for several years and after that they thought of having their own business instead of working under their masters.

And within no time the number of such workers who instead of working under their masters wanted to start their own business of running craft shops after gaining expertise, increased. Now their masters, to tackle this problem started a new system—'the franchise system'. The purpose of starting the franchise's system was to make certain regulations for the workers i.e. to regulate the workers in wage rate, their working hours etc.

After the application of franchise's system, the workers became more disappointed because this system of strict rules was unfavourable for them and hence it made the situation more complicated. As the number of such people had already gotten increased and they wanted to have the business of their own, they raised their voice against the prevailing system which resulted in the formation of 'labour unions'.

With the passage of time, the need was felt to start a school or a vocational educational program where the people who were willing to learn such type of skills can be taught and hence the increasing demand can be met. These schools used to provide training to skilled workers. Hence, it became easy for the people to learn new skills.

After that time period, the machines were introduced. The introduction of machines in the late 18th century was beneficial in the sense that it would help in producing more goods in less time but on the other hand it was disappointing for the skilled workers because they did not know how to use the machines. It was noticed that semi-skilled workers can produce well as compared to skilled workers.

Accepting the new method of doing work with the help of machines was very difficult for the workers.

It is a well-known fact that resistance to change is always there. It is the human nature that makes it difficult to accept the change in working methods. However, workers started working with machines but now to meet the demand, more machines were required and as a result, demand for the workers who can design and make machines increased.

And this was the time when it was required to start factory schools where mechanists and workers in other related areas could be developed.

People working under factory system were being exploited as they were treated as machines and not as workers. Their health conditions, wage rules, working conditions were also not good and they were required to work for long hours but were getting paid meagrely.

All the above mentioned factors made the workers dissatisfied and disappointed. So they no more wanted to continue working under the same system. This resulted in the start of 'human relations movement'.

2.3 Goals of HRD

Defining HRD goals is not an easy task rather it is a complicated one due to its complex nature as it requires inclusion of a lot of different activities, i.e. education, training, organization development, career development, process improvement, coaching, counselling etc.

However, some common basic goals can be as follows:
1. To recognize the capability of the employees with respect to jobs that they are doing presently and assessing future job requirements accordingly.
2. Training and development is an ongoing process. So, it is one of the major goals of HRD to carry it on continuously in order to get better employee performance and enhanced development.
3. To improve quality of employees and retain that improved quality in the organization as the need of best talent is always there.
4. To develop team spirit in employees and maximize learning opportunities for the employees working in the organization.
5. To apply time management and change development plans properly in the organization because there is always resistance to adapt to any change but sometimes change

becomes necessary for the development of business as well as its employees. Bringing the change, taking into consideration the time factor is the most important thing which has to be done very carefully.
6. To prepare the new staff to work for excellence according to expectations.
7. To promote the culture of respect, creativity, dignity, innovation and human development by telling employees in the organization to be creative, innovative and to maintain overall health of the organization. Also, the employees should be provided sufficient opportunities to develop.
8. To meet industrial and social obligations by contributing towards excellence.

2.4 Functions and Scope of HRD

The main purpose of HRD is to increase employee productivity and profitability. Keeping this in mind, HRD performs the following functions:

2.4.1 Training, Education and Development: To improve employee competency and the performance of an organization, the management needs to provide to its employees training, education and development opportunities at regular intervals whenever required. To provide these things to its employees is a continuous process in order to develop the employees and organization as a whole.

2.4.2 Training: Training is a short-term process provided to employees to improve their job performance. Many reputed companies spend a lot of money in providing training to its employees. Training helps in improving the productivity and to maintain the level and intensity of competitiveness among the businesses.

2.4.3 Education: Education helps the employees in learning new skills and enhancing knowledge which can help the employees to perform different tasks if he gets the opportunity. As compared to training, education is a long-term process.

2.4.4 Development: It is a long-term process using a systematic procedure by which managerial personnel learn conceptual and theoretical knowledge. It is neither restricted to the current job or future job but towards an overall growth of the employee and the organization.

Besides improving job performance, it also improves an employee's personality.

The main idea behind providing timely training to the employees is that it will help in increasing their knowledge and skills which would further result in the quality of work and the productivity i.e. the ratio of output to input. With the change in technology and increase in complexity, the companies have to compete in order to survive in such a rapidly changing global business environment. To improve the skills and knowledge of its employees and to make them grow, the companies invest a lot of amount in their training and development activities which ultimately helps in increasing organizational profitability.

2.5 Organizational Development

The main focus here in organizational development is to improve and enhance the capabilities within the organization to meet tactical and strategic goals. To develop an organization as a whole, attention is paid to employee motivation, group dynamics, behaviour, skills, values, performance management etc.

By creating and reinforcing training programs whenever required, the training process aims at bringing a systematic change in attitudes, value system and the beliefs of employees which further helps in adapting better to the changing external business environment. As training helps in building values system, attitudes and beliefs, the employees feel ready to cope with internally as well as externally changing business environment.

As we already know that there is always resistance to a change among the employees who are already working by following certain methods for a long time. They always resist

HRD: Importance, Emergence and Goals

to change because the old method of doing things is felt more comfortable to them rather than the new method e.g., introduction of computers in the business world made them feel insecure and hence there was resistance to change (to adopt computers in place of doing work manually). But there should be a proper change management system in the organization so that it becomes a little bit easier for the employees to go with the change. Employees were provided computer training so that they could learn working on the computers. It was really a revolutionary kind of thing to bring computers in the market. For proper application of the change, leaders are expected to play a bigger role in a planned way. A leader having good leadership qualities would help in bringing the desired change by taking into consideration the given time without making the process much complicated.

Talent management in the organization has become a very important area in human resource development. Talent has to be retained in an organization. Companies do a lot of efforts to retain the talent in an organization right from motivating them, offering them lucrative packages to providing them sufficient opportunities to grow. Nowadays, employees who have the talent, not only want a good package of salary and other benefits but they also need their continuous growth because in the current changing business environment, if someone wants to survive, he has to face the competition and this can be done with an employee's growth in various areas.

2.6 Career Development

This is an ongoing process which includes career planning and career management.

Career development involves managing the career either within the organization or between the organizations including learning new skills, improving employee skill set which helps in learning more and achieving more in the career. It is directly related to goals and objectives set by an individual who start with self-actualization after self-assessing his interest and capabilities.

Career planning is a process to identify one's knowledge, skill set, strengths and weakness in order to set the objectives to be achieved. Every employee wants to grow well in an organization where he is working. He wants everything to be increased whether it is his salary or his knowledge.

It is a process of setting his career objectives/goals and the path to achieve those goals. The main objective of career planning is to help the employees to get a good match between their own personal goals and the type of opportunities available to them in the organization.

It is a process of analyzing an individual's potential for promotion in the future keeping in mind his aspirations with organizational needs and opportunities. One of the main functions of career planning is to see whether the right type of employees (with the skills required) is available at the right time and at the right place in an organization or not.

2.7 Factors Affecting HRD

When we talk about human resources and their development, the first major thing is the person who is dealing with the human resources in any organization who should have proper knowledge of behavioural sciences which deals with human action (i.e. observing human action patterns of response to the external stimuli). Hence, having knowledge of behavioural science while dealing with human resources, helps in knowing their actions and reactions when a particular task or case is assigned to them.

This is important for the trainer to have this knowledge so that based on employee behaviour, he can successfully run his training by selecting appropriate training methods which are helpful for the employees to learn the subject matter easily.

Generalists and specialists should also be fully involved in this process so that the operating issues as well as the potential issues can be taken care of at the right time. Also, there should also be an alternative course of action which can be introduced to solve the current issue and proper solutions or plans should be made to avoid the re-occurrence of similar issues in the near future. Advancement in technology these days requires every employee to have the latest knowledge, gaining of which helps in an employee's growth. Nowadays, the employees themselves want to learn more through the training programs to add up more to their existing knowledge and skills which increases the level of productivity and helps in reducing obsolescence in the organization and further helps them to accept the challenges. Also the increased knowledge and improved skills help them in getting attractive salary packages. On the other hand, from the organizations' point of view, it wants to introduce advanced technology into the organization so that it can face the market competition and successfully earn sufficient profits.

In order to run a HRD programme in an organization, the full support of management is required. If the management is not willing to support it completely, it cannot be successful rather it would result in wastage of time, money and efforts of other employees engaged in it.

2.8 HRD Dimensions

Human resource development has different dimensions which are made to attain the required level of performance and to develop human resources in an organization.

An employee's cognitive capacities, capabilities and behaviour are the three dimensions of HRD being discussed here. These three elements are required in every organization.

All the above mentioned abilities or skills reflect his ability to understand, remember, analyze and evaluate a situation before giving it a final decision. All these qualities are equally important. Hence, an employee equipped with all these qualities is preferred to be hired and retained in an organization. And from the employee's point of view also, it is important for him to have problem-solving ability, reasoning ability, decision-making ability, creativity, skills to memorize, problem analyzing skills etc. to be successful in any business organization because it does not just tell how smart the employees are but also it tells how well is their brain functioning etc. (how correctly they understand the information and after understanding it how is it being processed and finally how well they can recall that information).

Properly understanding the information is one important function of the brain as it leads to the process of information which is the other important function and then recalling that information at right time is again necessary as an organization requires its employees to be good at information understanding, processing and recalling.

Now talking about intelligent quotient, level of IQ required to perform a specific job depends upon the level of complexity of the job i.e. if it is less complex, a lesser level of IQ will work and vice versa.

Cognitive capacities are necessary to process the information and gain knowledge which is further helpful in an overall development of employee and the organization as a whole.

3

Meaning and Approaches to Organizational Effectiveness

In simple words, we can say that a group of people working together towards the achievement of common goals represent an organization. Hence, they work for achieving some pre-determined goals which is the first step in the process of organization. Based on the objectives to be achieved, activities to be performed are divided into different parts so that the appropriate/right person is assigned the right kind of job to perform. All the people working in an organization coordinate with others and develop their relationships.

To run an organization, organization structure is formed which defines how different activities i.e. allocation of different tasks, coordination and supervision are directed to achieve the pre-determined goals.

An organization is a consciously coordinated social unit, composed of two or more people that function on a relatively continuous basis to achieve the common goals.

An organization is required to be effective in order to get the best out of it. To define effectiveness is difficult as it means different to different persons and due to this there are problems with finding its measures too.

3.1 Organizational Effectiveness Defined

Only executive effectiveness can enable this society of ours to harmonize its two needs: the needs of an organization to obtain from the individual, the contribution of its needs and the needs of the individual to have organization serve as his tool for accomplishing his purposes.

A great deal of behaviour and particularly behaviour of the individuals within administrative organizations is purposive-oriented towards goals and objectives. This purposiveness bring about an integration in the pattern of the behaviour, in the absence of which administration will be meaningless, for if administration consists in getting things done by a group of people, purpose provides a principal criterion in determining what are the things to be done.

Organizational effectiveness captures organizational performance plus the myriad internal performance outcomes normally associated with more efficient or effective operations and other external measures that relate to considerations that are broader than those simple associated with economic valuation (either be shareholders, managers or customers), such as corporate social responsibility.

Effectiveness is the degree of the congruence between goals of the organization and some observed outcomes. How effectively an organization is achieving the outcomes which it aimed to produce is known as organizational effectiveness. In other words, organizational effectiveness is the extent to which, with given resources and means, an organization achieves its goals.

An organization can be effective or ineffective in a number of different ways which may be relatively independent of each other:
- Productivity.
- Efficiency.
- Employees' absenteeism.
- Goals consensus.
- Competitiveness.
- Participation in decision-making.
- Survival.
- Turnover.
- Communication.
- Conflict.
- Stability.
- Satisfaction.
- Flexibility.
- Quality.

Criteria of organizational effectiveness are listed in Table 3.1.

Table 3.1: Criteria of Organizational Effectiveness

Stakeholder	Criteria
Owners	Financial return
Employees	Job satisfaction (work conditions, salary etc.)
Government	To follow laws properly (rules/regulations)
Credit	Credit worthiness
Customers	Satisfaction (product/service price and quality)
Community	Contributions towards its affairs

Organizational effectiveness works on continuously improving the performance of the organization, its capacity and the outcomes. It is not concerned with specific unit of an organization but with the entire organization. An effective organization can be observed as an operating system which is made up of the following components:
- Strategy.
- Inputs.
- Performance capacity.
- Performance actions.
- Outcomes.
- Feedback.

3.2 Organizational System

Formulation of strategy is the primary responsibility of the senior managers which is based on matching the skills, resources, values of the people working in an organization towards the needs and expectations of the people outside the organization.

External as well as internal environment affects strategy formulation and organizational design which leads to the outcomes. Inputs are the resources which have been procured by the organization from the environment e.g., finance, people, materials, equipment, etc.

Performance capacity is the ability of an organization to

use the resources and hence contribute its best to the outcomes. Performance capacity includes budget capacity, workforce capacity, etc.

Performance actions are the actions towards the outcomes. These actions include product development, services etc. Output is the system's performance results.

Organizational alignment is the most important feature of an effective organization. Effective organizations put focus and a lot of efforts to make and maintain the alignment in different but interconnected parts of an organization. In order to make the parts effective, their roles need to be expanded to increase their impact on efforts heading towards organizational effectiveness.

3.3 Approaches to Measure Organizational Effectiveness

The resources which are required by the organizations are brought into the organizations from the environment and after transforming them into the outputs, they are delivered back to the environment. Following are the different approaches to measure the organizational effectiveness.

3.3.1 System Resource Approach: The system resource approach measures the effectiveness of an organization by observing the process at the starting and then making an evaluation "how effectively resources were obtained". Hence, it can be said that the ability to obtain the scarce and valuable resources from the environment is known as organizational effectiveness as per system resource approach.

Indicators of effectiveness in resource approach include the following:
- Ability of the decision-makers in the organization to correctly interpret the environment.
- Organization's ability to respond to the changing environment.
- Organization's ability to acquire the scarce resources from external environment (by bargaining etc.).

3.3.2 Internal Process Approach: How effectively the

resources are being used and coordinated internally in an organization, is measured under the internal process approach to gauge an organization's effectiveness. According to this approach, the ability to excel at internal efficiency, harmonious internal functioning, motivation and employee satisfaction is known as effectiveness. This approach is used when the output costs and the satisfaction are easily measurable. The indicators of effectiveness as per this approach are as under:

- Positive work climate.
- Teamwork, trust and confidence.
- Loyalty and team spirit.
- Strong corporate culture.
- Managers get rewards for growth of subordinates and effective groups.
- Proper communication between workers and management.

3.3.3 Goal Approach: Whether the desired levels of output have been achieved or not is taken into consideration under the goal approach. It is the ability to excel at output goals. This approach is used when the goals to be attained are clear, measurable and have a given time period.

The approaches mentioned above have their own shortcomings.

The *system resource approach* has the shortcomings too as often to obtain the resources from the external environment seem less important than utilizing the resources.

In *internal process approach*, the evaluation of functioning and internal health is often subjective because there are so many aspects of the internal processes and inputs which cannot be measured.

The g*oals approach* is mostly used in the business organization because the output can be measured here in terms of growth, profitability, market share, etc.

3.3.4 Competing Value Model: This approach has the opinion that an organization performs various activities and also it has different and competing viewpoints about the constituents of effectiveness. To contribute to the solution to this problem, Quinn and Rohr Baugh developed Competing Values Model. According to this, organizational focus and organizational structure are the broad dimensions.

Dimension 1: Organizational Focus: It concerns about the dominant values, i.e. whether the issues are internal or external to the organization.

- **Internal Focus:** It is a concern for employee well-being and efficiency.
- **External Focus:** It reflects an emphasis on the organizational well-being and its 'fit' with the environment.

Dimension 2: Organizational Structure: It concerns about stability vs. flexibility which is the dominant value in an organization.

- **Stability:** It reflects concern for the top-down control and efficiency.
- **Flexibility**: It represents learning and change.

3.4 Steer's Multi-dimensional Perspective

Steer (1977) developed a multi-dimensional perspective which is a three-tier approach emphasizing the following:
- Goal optimization.
- System perspective.
- Behavioural emphasis.

3.4.1 Goal Optimization: In his opinion, effectiveness is the capacity of an organization to obtain the required scarce resources and their utilization as expeditiously as possible. Here, the constraints (identifiable and irreducible) are recognized first, which makes it possible to identify the resulting goals. It helps in evaluating effectiveness in terms of how well an organization's feasible goals can be attained as against the desired ones.

3.4.2 System Perspective: It takes into consideration various factors affecting the goal directed efforts.

3.4.3 Behavioural Emphasis: It is the behaviour of the employees which contributes to the organizational success. Hence, it emphasizes on the role of employee behaviour in organizational success.

Productivity is a major issue being faced by the organizations. In simple terms, we can say that productivity is the ratio of output to input. Hence, it includes both the quantity as well as quality of work. The two major factors with which productivity is concerned include organizational effectiveness and organizational efficiency.

3.5 Time Dimensional Model

Time dimension model, which is based on system theory, was developed by Ivancevich and Matterson in 2002. As described in the system theory, the input-output cycle and interrelationship between an organization and the environment must be reflected by the organizational effectiveness criteria.

Organizations have life cycles consisting of different stages i.e. growth, development, decline and as per this model, the effectiveness criteria should reflect life cycle stages. To access the long-run survival probability, there are various indicators which include productivity, efficiency, quality, turnover etc.

3.6 Cameron's Four-criterion Measure

Cameron (1980 and 1986) developed a four-criterion model to measure an organization's effectiveness. This measure of effectiveness can be used in different combinations. It is based on four approaches which are as follows:
- Goal approach.
- Resource acquisition approach.
- Internal process approach.
- Strategic constituencies' satisfaction approach.

According to *goal approach*, if an organization meets its goals, it is considered to be effective.

If an organization is able to acquire the resources it needs from the environment, it is deemed effective as per the *resource acquisition approach*.

If in an organization, there is a smooth flow of information, and employees are loyal, committed and satisfied, it is deemed to be effective as per the *internal process approach*.

If an organization processes the ability to satisfy the strategic constituents, it is deemed to be effective according to the *strategic constituencies' satisfaction approach*.

3.7 Social Function Model

This model was developed by Talcott Parsons (1960) who suggested that all social systems must solve the following four basic problems:

- **Goal Achievement:** Here, the objectives must be properly defined first and then resources must be properly mobilized towards the attainment to those objectives.
- **Integration**: There must be established and organized member units in a system so that these can be well coordinated towards a single entity.
- **Adaptation:** How well the system accommodates to the environmental demands? In other words, it can be said that it is the management's ability to sense organizational as well as environmental changes and based on that how well it responds.
- **Latency:** It describes how well the motivational as well as cultural patterns have been maintained in an organization.

Hence, being a social system, an organization is expected to resolve all these problems in order to be effective as per this model.

3.8 Robey and Sales Integrated Four Way Approach

Robey and Sales (1994) developed an integrated four way approach to measure the organizational effectiveness. The four approaches used in this model are:
- Output goal approach.
- Internal process approach.
- System process.
- Stakeholder approach.

The *output goal approach* focuses on the end results whereas the *internal process approach* emphasizes on maintaining human relations effectively.

The *system resource approach* concerns about "how well the resources are obtained from the environment".

Stakeholder approach emphasises on satisfying internal and external group's demands (How well their demands are being satisfied).

In this model, different arguments are made regarding first three approaches as those approaches are based on what is important for an organization but the fourth approach (i.e. the stakeholder approach) seeks to balance the multiple biases provided by other three approaches.

3.9 Job Analysis

It is always important for an organization as well as for employees to know what job/tasks are being performed by an employee at a given position which includes the duties and responsibilities etc. of that employee (which is known as job description). This term is still in use in some organizations. However, later on, the need was felt to provide more attention to this area and as a result "job analysis" was introduced.

Jobs are expected to be properly designed and rightly performed. If they are not, it adversely affects an organization's productivity, profit, customer's level of satisfaction, demand of employees and other stakeholders. So, in an organization, a job should be properly defined in terms of its components i.e. tasks, knowledge or skill-set etc. required to perform it, which is generally done by performing a job analysis.

"The data generated by job analysis has significant use in nearly every phase of human resource administration viz. designing jobs and reward systems, staffing and training, performance control and more. Few other processes executed by organizations have the potential for being such a powerful aid for management's decision-making"—*Philips C. Grant.*

4

Knowledge Management: Dimensions and Tools

Knowledge management is the identification and mapping of intellectual assets within an organization, the creation of knowledge for competitive advantage, the conversion of vast amounts of available corporate data into accessible information and the distribution of best practices.

Before understanding the concept of knowledge management, it becomes necessary first to understand the interrelationship between *data* and *information*.

Data are raw facts which are unprocessed and unorganized. *Information* is the processed data which is meaningful and hence can be understood by the person who receives it. For example, if the numbers 24 and 1 are given, it will be of no use to us because it does not mean much. So, at this level, these are data. But if we are given 24 as (hours) in 1 day instead of only 24, then it becomes meaningful and understandable. Now it has become information. Hence, it can be said that it is important to create/understand a relationship between the given data to make it an *information*.

4.1 Knowledge Management Defined

Being the most valuable asset of an organization, managing knowledge has become crucial in this knowledge competitive world.

We may not be thinking in terms of knowledge management but in one way or other we are doing it. For example, an employee xyz is working in a company and simultaneously he is pursuing further education and the company is extending him some type of motivation either by increasing his salary or promoting him to higher level to do this. In this case, an employee and the company both may not be thinking in terms of knowledge management but knowingly or unknowingly they are doing it because peoples' knowledge is the most important asset of an organization and they want to develop it in order to avoid any kind of risk in the present competitive scenario and for their own development. On the other side, company is motivating people to gain more knowledge as it wants to retain knowledge and develop it in the organization because peoples' knowledge is the intellectual asset of a company.

"Knowledge management is the way organizations create, capture, enhance, and reuse knowledge to achieve organizational objectives"—*Asian Development Bank.*

"Knowledge management is a collection of activities, processes and policies, which enable organizations to apply knowledge, to improve effectiveness, innovation and quality"— *UN Knowledge Management Workshop.*

"Knowledge is power, which is why people who had it in the past often tried to make a secret of it. In post-capitalism, power comes from transmitting information to make it productive, not from hiding it!"—*Peter Drucker.*

"Knowledge management is a process that emphasizes on generating, capturing and sharing information know how and integrating these into business practices and decision-making for greater organizational benefit"—*Maggie Haines.*

"Knowledge management is not about data, but about getting the right information to the right people at the right time for them to impact the bottom line"—*IBM.*

"Knowledge management is the explicit and systematic management of vital knowledge and its associated processes of creating, gathering, organizing, diffusion, use and exploitation. It requires turning personal knowledge into corporate knowledge that can be widely shared throughout an organization and appropriately applied"—*David J. Skyrme.*

New idea in the whole concept of knowledge management is the "knowledge of people". Using/transferring knowledge does not mean losing it. There are lots of sources of getting knowledge i.e. discussing it with others, reading magazines, through internet, etc. There is no scarcity of the knowledge but there is lack of ability to use it. So, here knowledge management is concerned about using the right type of knowledge at the right place at the right time.

4.2 Importance of Knowledge Management

For an organization to run smoothly and for its own development as well as for the development of its employees', knowledge management has become very important in the present business scenario which is discussed as follows:

- **Less Chances of Repetition of Previous Mistakes:** With the feedback provided to an employee regarding his previous work, he would take care while doing the same task next time.
- **Relevant and Effective Work:** Knowledge management helps in reducing the chance of error which helps in making work effective resulting in time saving.
- **Strong Network among Employees:** Knowledge management creates a strong network among its employees as they get an opportunity to share their experiences and knowledge with others which further helps them to develop new ideas and it improves their problem solving skills.
- **Creates Atmosphere of Learning and Sharing:** Accessibility to knowledge when required helps the employees in solving their problems and also the transfer of knowledge helps employees in gaining knowledge. Employees feel motivated when they get some reward and recognition for sharing knowledge which helps in creating atmosphere of learning and sharing knowledge which helps in employee as well as organizational development.
- **Helps in Finding Common Issues and Challenges:** With the experiences of the employees, knowledge management helps in finding the common issues and challenges for the

organization which further helps in finding the ways to overcome such issues for the smooth running of the business.

4.3 Types of Knowledge

Experience gained by an individual from the type of work he/she is doing, his studies, his expertise, his influences on attitude of other individuals, reflects his knowledge.

There are two types of knowledge:
1. Tacit knowledge, and
2. Explicit knowledge.

4.3.1 Tacit Knowledge: It has following characteristics:
- Based on experience.
- Personal, stored in the heads of people.
- Gained through study and experience.
- Develops through communication with others.
- Difficult to transfer, record because it cannot be easily expressed or written.

We understand and we are aware but we find it difficult to express everything regarding that what we are having in our mind but we can easily express it with the help of demos, workshops, on-job training, etc. because it is scarce and unique, highly individualized. Sharing with others depends upon the willingness of the person having it plus his ability to communicate with others.

4.3.2 Explicit Knowledge: It can be coded and documented which can further be stored in databases, websites, email and it can also take the form of procedures, policies and research reports. Where tacit knowledge is about learning/adapting new things, explicit knowledge concerns with the ability to disseminate and reapply. It is the ability to teach/track. So, here we can see that where tacit knowledge is personal, in case of explicit knowledge once it is made explicit (i.e. codified) it does not belong to the individual, rather the organization becomes the owner of it. Hence, an organization can further make that knowledge available to all the employees working in the organization for the sake of betterment of the organization.

But on the other hand, these two types of knowledge are complementary in nature too. If an individual lacks tacit knowledge, it will become difficult for him to understand explicit knowledge and vice-versa. For example, a person who lacks in tacit knowledge, cannot understand the complex diagrams which are technical in nature and in the same way he cannot convert tacit into explicit knowledge. For example, if the explicit knowledge (in the form of procedures, documents, memos, reports, etc.) is available, neither he can study it nor can he discuss it with others.

If we cannot convert the knowledge that we have inside our head into explicit knowledge, others cannot understand it, they cannot comment it or discuss it as it is out of their reach and is not adding value to the organization taken as a whole.

4.4 SECI Model of Knowledge Dimensions

This model of knowledge transfer was developed by Nonaka and Takeuchi which is known as SECI (socialization, externalisation, combination and internalization) model of knowledge creation.

- **Tacit-to-tacit (Socialization):** Through socialization, transfer of knowledge takes place by face to face communication and discussions about employees' experiences in their gatherings. Tacit knowledge can be acquired if people are living in the same type of environment, spending time together and sharing their experiences. This type of transfer of knowledge is called tacit to tacit knowledge transfer.
- **Tacit-to-explicit (Externalisation):** By publishing knowledge and making it available to other people, this type of knowledge transfer takes place. One way to transfer this type of knowledge is by publishing in magazines, documents, emails etc. and making it available to others. This is called externalisation.
- **Explicit-to-explicit (Combination):** It is a combination of

different type of explicit knowledge from inside the organization or outside the organization. After the combination, it is edited wherever required and processed further and then it is made available to the employees of the organization.
- **Explicit-to-tacit (Internalization):** It involves receiving knowledge and applying it practically. This process of gaining knowledge is called internalization. It is useful for both employees as well as the organization as for an organization, this transfer of knowledge becomes an asset and for an employee, it enhances his knowledge.

After internalization, this process goes on and on as it is a spiral of knowledge creation.

4.5 Knowledge Management Process

The process of knowledge management starts with discovering the knowledge first then creating it and after creating knowledge, it is stored and shared with the others.

4.5.1 Knowledge Capture/Creation: Knowledge can be captured or created by using capture tools such as programs, books, articles and experts etc. from outside the organization as well as inside the organization. Tacit knowledge can be added by discussions, meetings etc. in an organization. Usually, there is management interference when it comes to creating knowledge which should be the least so that the process of creating knowledge can flourished and that is the reason this part of knowledge management is called the toughest part.

When we find out or identify the knowledge by developing new tacit knowledge or explicit knowledge from the given data/information or with the help of our prior knowledge it is termed as capturing the knowledge. This knowledge may reside inside or outside the organization (including employees, experts, customers, competitors, suppliers etc.).

4.5.2 Codifying and Testing of Knowledge: It involves codifying the knowledge into tables, shells, maps rules etc.

which is further tested for logic, user acceptance, training etc. so that it is easily understood by the people. It is an important part of the knowledge management process to codify the knowledge properly and to test it further logically and for user acceptance so that people can easily understand the knowledge when presented to them.

4.5.3 Sharing and Transferring Knowledge: Sharing of knowledge is a process which includes tacit or explicit knowledge to be shared with other individuals or employees in the organization by using collaborative tools, networks, intranets. For knowledge sharing, employees should have easy and direct access, instead of following the long route of going through higher management level whenever they need information or knowledge which is further required in implementing the projects.

But somehow, nowadays, people do not want to share their knowledge because they believe that knowledge is power and if they share their knowledge with the other employees in the organization, their power is lost. This thinking arises due to lack of trust in other individuals and a fear factor related to this is always there which says that the other one to whom the employee is going to share the knowledge may start getting the credit by using that knowledge.

4.6 Knowledge Management Barriers

Management of knowledge is an important task for an organization but in practice we see some barriers in the path of knowledge management which needs to be overcome. The main barriers are discussed below.

4.6.1 Lack of Technical Infrastructure: IT helps in applying knowledge management successfully. So, its lack becomes a major barrier in the path of knowledge management. This information technology infrastructure includes computer networks, DBM devices, data centres, computer networks and transmission media.

Hence, the lack of IT infrastructure in an organization

becomes a hindrance in successful development of knowledge management in an organization.

4.6.2 Lack of Organizational Structure: Task forces are made up of employees who are experts in specific areas who work together to attain broad business objectives. Task forces are created on need basis. In knowledge management, this type of organization structure is helpful as compared to bureaucratic organization structure because in bureaucratic organization structure, formal structure exists, which limits an individual's decisions. Here, a little creativity is allowed and also a very little chance of deviations from the already set norms is allowed. Importance is given to the structure as an organizational structure is strictly followed and the power is concentrated in few hands of top ranking professionals. Hence, bureaucratic organization hinders the free flow of knowledge into the organization and should be avoided.

On the other hand, a task force structure should be adopted due to its flexibility and also here people work together to find out the causes and solutions to the problems.

4.6.3 Lack of Organizational Culture: Organizational culture is made up of beliefs, norms, values, attitudes, expectations and behaviour of its people. The above mentioned factors influence their decision-making and action taking which has an effect on company's well-being in one way or the other. If an organization lacks in organizational culture, there cannot be a successful implementation of knowledge management. Because in such a scenario, employees would not like to share their knowledge as there is an absence of team spirit.

4.6.4 Lack of Motivation: Lack of motivation is another barrier in the implementation of knowledge management in an organization. If there is no motivation, there is no recognition and hence no knowledge sharing. If people are timely noted and motivated for the type of good work they do, it encourages them to do better next time but if there is no motivation when they are sharing knowledge, they would stop sharing it or avoid it as they think that they are in a neutral state. It is same when they were not sharing and now when they have shared brings no change. Hence, it hinders the flow of knowledge into an organization.

4.6.5 Expertise Retirement: It becomes very difficult to replace a retiring employee with a substitute with the same level of expertise. Here, the organizations are required to develop a system of retaining/transferring the knowledge in their organization and hence protecting their intellectual capital. To maintain that level of knowledge is very important when a person retires and a manager should be more concerned about retaining that knowledge.

4.6.6 Lack of Time: Due to lack of time, implementing knowledge management in an organization becomes difficult. Sometimes due to pressure of work and rigid organizational structure, employees do not find sufficient time to avail the opportunity to share knowledge. And also it becomes very difficult to know who needs what type of knowledge because they are not aware of that kind of information due to lack of time.

4.6.7 Fear of Sharing Knowledge: Employees have fear of sharing knowledge because they think that sharing knowledge can put them in a state of risk which can be related to their job security or position, etc. Here, such type of situation brings a major barrier while implementing knowledge management in an organization. Fear of sharing knowledge has to be removed and it is a cause of concern. Hence, employees should be encouraged more to share knowledge by giving them timely motivation such as rewards, recognition, etc. It helps them in sharing more knowledge.

4.6.8 Lack of Proper Feedback: Proper feedback is must for the employees as it is the source of knowing quality of work that they are doing. Lack of proper feedback creates barrier in implementation of knowledge management. Also, some employees do not tolerate the feedback given to them about their past mistakes. This also contributes to knowledge management barrier.

4.7 Knowledge Management Tools and Techniques

These are as follows:

4.7.1 Case Study: Doing a project's detailed examination helps in knowing the information i.e. qualitative as well as quantitative which is further helpful in the application of knowledge management into the business. Here, the team which is undergoing a case study records the best methods/ practices so that it can be conveyed to other employees who require such type of information. Findings based on case study are one of the important tools of knowledge management. Based on the findings, employees are informed about the main problems, the methods/practices which help in solving problems etc. They are also informed about the best way to solve the problem so that they can keep that thing in mind while solving the related problems in future which may help in time and cost saving.

4.7.2 Community Interaction: People having common interests or problems get together virtually or face-to-face to discuss their issues, solutions and best practices to solve their problems. This tool of knowledge management provides a better understanding of problems and solutions. Also, it increases their social network as it helps in forming informal groups which gather to solve their common problems or fulfil their common needs. These days, technology provides various online facilities to share common interests or problems.

In this tool of knowledge management, experienced peers are asked for ideas/suggestions which is required to solve one's problems. It is a time and cost saving process as the peers who are being consulted are experts in the same area in which the assistance is required.

4.7.3 Rapid Evidence Review: This is the next important tool used in implementing knowledge management. In rapid evidence review, the main outcomes of the researches already done are recorded so that it can be of some help when starting some new task/project in the same area. It is called 'rapid' as it is the quickest way of getting knowledge from the findings of the researches already done.

In this method, people are gathered who have done work in the area in which help/knowledge is required. Now, they can be asked to give ideas regarding the current problem. Discussions can be done based on ideas provided by them.

4.7.4 Knowledge Café: Here, the people having interests in mutual topics are invited for an open discussion.

These type of discussions help in creating new ideas, getting new knowledge, new problem solving methods, expert's suggestions and the latest information about the topic, which ultimately helps in one way or another in adding up to the existing knowledge and hence solving the problem.

4.7.5 Feedback: Taking feedback of an activity or event when it is done is another important knowledge management tool as it helps in getting open views as well as critical views or other new ideas on how to do a particular task in a better way. The good as well as bad points of the event are noted so that next time while maintaining the good points, one can improve upon bad points too.

4.7.6 Retrospective Review: *After* a project is completed, a detailed discussion takes place which helps in retaining the knowledge that has been just gained and also helps in clearing all the doubts/confusion regarding that specific project. Areas which were covered in good way and other which need improvement are also taken care of. This tool helps in gaining detailed knowledge on a specific issue.

4.7.7 Brainstorming: This pertains to an activity of generating a group of ideas which are gathered from different people to make a final conclusion based on their ideas.

This is done by conveying the problem to all the individuals participating in brainstorming and they are asked to provide their ideas or solutions. Then all the ideas are gathered and analyzed on a theme and then a final conclusion is made. This method is useful when there is a need to generate more ideas or opinions in order to select the best one.

4.7.8 Taxonomy: It is a technique to organize information already stored in the documents, libraries etc. in a consistent way so that it can be easily accessed by the individuals who need it. Here, an organization of information is based on a specific sequence or hierarchy of concepts/terms etc. It helps the staff in accessing the required information about the organization very quickly without wasting huge amount of valuable time.

4.7.9 Knowledge Audit: It is a kind of qualitative evaluation which is done by investigating the knowledge in the organization by knowing the needs of the organization and the type of knowledge assets an organization is already having as it helps in knowing the amount of gap in knowledge required. By doing so, it becomes helpful for an organization to know what type of knowledge is required by its employees and what type of knowledge they already have.

Knowledge should be accessible at the right time and at the right place. Moreover, knowledge audit helps in finding the hindrances in the flow of knowledge. If knowledge is getting stopped at a particular level, it needs to be unblocked to continue its flow.

4.7.10 Exit Interviews: These are the interviews taken of the employees who are leaving the organization to know the type of experience they had in an organization. This is basically a kind of feedback from the employees about the working system in the organization. Also, there must be some employees in the organization who might get the benefit from the knowledge of person leaving the organization.

Here, explicit knowledge can be taken from the documents, emails and files used by them. Explicit knowledge is easy to capture but tacit knowledge is not that easy. So, to get this tacit knowledge, a face to face interview is required and in the interview, questions should be prepared in advance as per the requirement.

4.7.11 Knowledge Harvesting: It is a process of capturing tacit knowledge from the experts and then to document it so that it can be made available to other employees in various different ways. It can be made available to employees through training, KM databases etc. Hence, this is the way of extracting knowledge from the brains of experts and making it available to other employees so that they make use of it by understanding it. Also, it is an art of the interviewer to extract the required knowledge from the heads of the experts. So, for the purpose of harvesting, a trained harvester (a trained interviewer) is required who knows how to take out right knowledge from the right person?

4.7.12 White Pages: It is a tool in an organization to find the expert who is having the same kind of knowledge which a person is looking for in order to solve the issue to accomplish a given task.

This is a type of directory having names of employees, their departments, rank, knowledge, experience etc. This tool is very helpful for the employees who are searching to gain knowledge in specific areas as per their job or task requirement in an organization.

5

Learning and HRD

Many of us often use the term 'to learn' to answer when somebody asks us: Why do you go to school? But what is really meant by this term? Let us find out.

We all are learning since our birth. Sometimes we learn by looking at others and while at other times, a teacher teaches us. A teacher assumes that students are learning because they are being taught and on the other hand students think that because they have heard the lecture, memorized the things, they have learnt. Learning occurs when new knowledge is gained or the existing one is modified due to experience.

Also, learning is a process of bringing together personal experiences and influences in order to gain, modify or enrich one's knowledge, value system, attitude, behaviour and skills.

5.1 Principles of Learning

The theories or principles involved in adult learning, provided by Knowles' (1984) theory of 'andragogy' and Kolb's (1984) learning style inventory are most accepted theories in the field of learning principles which conclude that adults are self-directed and they take responsibility for their own learning. Hence, their learning programme should be designed keeping into consideration the learning needs. They should be provided sufficient opportunities to learn by doing and take learning as a problem solving activity.

Principles of learning can be explained as follows:

5.1.1 Setting the Goals: There are some goals to be set for the trainer as well as for the learner. The trainer/teacher is expected to define the goals of providing training and learners should make the goals of their own e.g. after undergoing a particular training, what they will learn and how is it going to change their method of doing job. The setting of goals by learners helps them to feel motivated as well as encouraged which increases their level of interest and understanding.

5.1.2 Meaningful Presentation/Material: The material used in training should be properly organized. Each successive experience should build the preceding ones; this is how the material is required to be arranged. In this manner, it is helpful for the learners to integrate the experiences into a pattern of knowledge and skills which is going to be useable.

5.1.3 Transfer of Knowledge: In the process of learning, it is always required that there should be transfer of knowledge to some extent. As far as business is concerned, what is learnt should be applicable in practical life. The application of learning practically is the most important part of providing training and for that very purpose it becomes necessary to observe how trainees are doing keeping into consideration the work environment that supports and the consequent reinforcements to the employees for applying new skills and knowledge while doing their job. Also, there should be a proper plan of rewarding the employees who are contributing new skills and knowledge to the process so that they as well as other employees feel encouraged and motivated.

5.1.4 Individual Differences: While teaching in a class, a teacher may find different types of students having different learning patterns or methods. Likewise, some people working in an organization have different ways of learning. Some people can remember a given piece of information after hearing it once only. This type of memory is called 'echoic memory', while there is other group of people who can learn the things or grasp the information after looking at it only once. Those kinds of people are known to have 'iconic memory'. Apart from the above two types of different memory based groups, there is the other group of people who take a relatively long time to retrieve the information. In this category of people, there may be some other types of people having other than those already discussed e.g. people having hard time in learning in long lectures but they learn very well in small lectures/discussions.

Hence, in order to accommodate the differences in a given set of individuals, training programmes should be designed in a manner that supports learning among different types of people available.

5.1.5 Practice and Repetition: As the saying goes 'practice makes a man perfect', to gain any type of perfection whether theoretical or practical with the right type of tools and techniques, practice is always required. Also, practice brings confidence and a confident person always does much better than the non-confident one. Mere collection of theoretical knowledge is insufficient. For example, while performing the role of a typist in an organization, only knowing the pattern and positions of keys in the type writer without practicing on it, does not increase one's typing speed. It has to be done practically again and again and this repetition of practice will surely result in increased typing speed in the end.

Hence, in the same manner, the employees should be able to use the learnt information while performing their jobs and to make this possible, while providing them training they should be given sufficient opportunity to apply that knowledge and skills practically in the presence of instructors so that if they face any difficulty, they can ask the instructors for solutions.

5.1.6 Whole vs. Part Learning: There are some jobs and tasks that can be broken into different parts that lead them to further analysis. Then, the most effective manner to complete each part further provides a basis of providing a specific instructor. For example, while selling a car, the process of selling can be broken down into two parts:
1. Product knowledge—which involves knowing in depth the specifications of the product (car).
2. Need of customer—to know what customer needs, keeping in mind his budget to spend for a car.

Hence, in this example, there are two different types of topics which can be learnt separately. The first part is all about the product i.e. the car and the next part is all about knowing the customer's needs keeping in mind his budget. Combining these two will serve the required purpose. The basic idea behind whole vs. part learning is that it facilitates the process of learning.

5.1.7 Distributed Learning: Also known as mass vs. distributed learning, it favours providing small training sessions as compared to longer training sessions because it is observed that smaller the sessions, more is the learning retention and vice versa, e.g. providing training in 2 sessions of 2 hours each is better than 2 sessions of 3 hours each.

5.1.8 Multiple Sense Learning: Many researchers in the related field have reported that multiple sense learning (that involves different aids like audio, visual, etc.) improves learning quality. Hence, learning process completed by using mainly sight (visuals) and hearing (audio) are considered to be very important.

5.1.9 Feedback: As in the process of communication, which is considered to be incomplete without a feedback, the process of learning is also incomplete without its feedback because learning is impossible without a feedback. So, here in the process of learning, feedback is provided which helps to know the results and it also provides motivation. Feedback plays an important role as it further helps in making things correct e.g. when you learn driving a car by a trainer, he keeps observing you during the whole process and tells you where you did wrong and how you can improve it. So, here in the same manner, the ultimate purpose of providing feedback is to correct the incorrect part in order to complete the process of learning.

5.1.10 Reinforcement: Sometimes, you must have noticed or taken an exam where you did good and the instructor told you that you did good or better, and his response made you felt motivated. This is reinforcement. Hence, reinforcement is a way to strengthen the response of an employee. It is observed that the behaviour of an employee, who is rewarded (positively) helps him feel motivated and is exhibited more frequently in the future as compared to the behaviour which is unrewarded or penalized.

5.1.11 Use of Learning Curve: The progress of employee should be recorded after taking tests etc. and the progress is plotted on the map. It helps in increasing or maintaining the level of motivation. This process of plotting results in formation of a curve is known as 'learning curve'. Figure 5.1 shows a typical learning curve.

Figure 5.1: Learning Curve

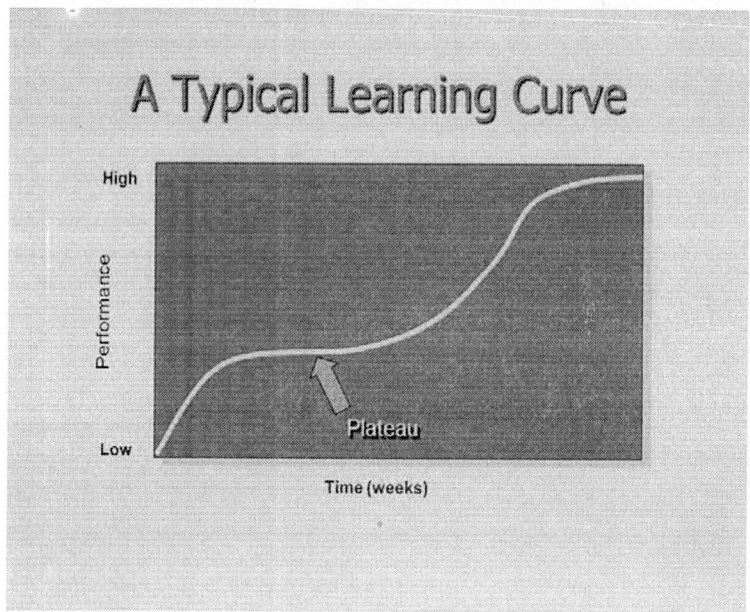

5.2 Kolb's Model of 4-stage Cycle of Adult Learning

Propounded by David A. Kolb, this model explains how people learn. He recognized learning as a cycle having four stages which are explained in Figure 5.2.

5.2.1 Active Experimentation: As depicted in Figure 5.2, this is the first stage of learning. It leads to other stages.

Figure 5.2: Kolb's Model of Learning

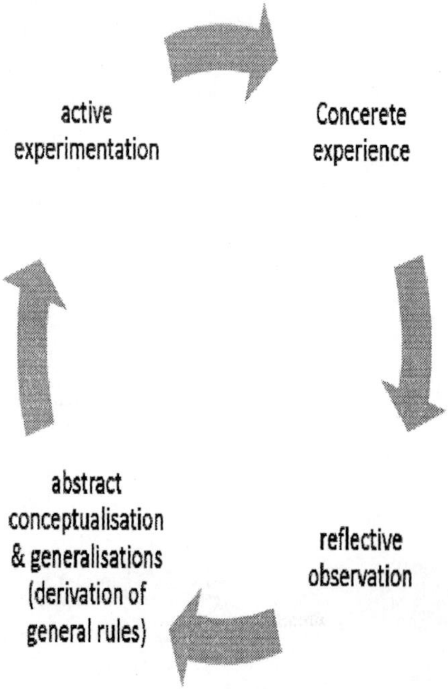

- active experimentation
- Concerete experience
- reflective observation
- abstract conceptualisation & generalisations (derivation of general rules)

5.2.2 Concrete Experience (CE): The presence of concrete experience in a person helps him to be involved completely, openly and with unbiased attitude in case of new experiences.

5.2.3 Reflective Observations (ROs): The presence of reflective observation (ability) in a person enables him to observe as well as reflect these experiences from many different perspectives.

5.2.4 Abstract Conceptualization (AC): The theories which a person makes using the above mentioned abilities should be competent enough to apply those theories in decision-making and problem solving. The presence of this ability in a learner is known as active experimentation ability.

5.3 Theories of Learning

Different authors came up with different types of learning

theories after doing a lot of research work in the related area. However, the most influential learning theories are explained as follows.

5.3.1 Behaviourism: This theory was introduced by John B. Watson and B.F. Skinner. It is based upon the principle of "stimulus response" which means the behaviour that is caused by external stimuli. The change in behaviour due to acquiring, reinforcing and applying associations between stimuli and the individual is considered as learning according to the behaviourists.

Basic assumptions of this theory:
1. Learner is passive in responding to external stimuli.
2. The way he is going to behave:
- Positive reinforcement, and
- Negative reinforcement.

Here, positive reinforcement means the application whereas the negative reinforcement means stopping of stimuli. Both types of reinforcement indicate that antecedent behaviour is going to happen again and change in the behaviour is the outcome of learning.

According to behaviourists, learning is the acquisition of new behaviour. This theory of learning is the theory of animal and human learning with a focus on their behaviour and it discounts their mental activities.

Based on their experiments, behaviourists found 'conditioning' as a universal learning process. It is further explained as follows.

5.3.2 Ivan Pavlov's Dog Theory: A noted Russian physiologist, Ivan Pavlov won the Nobel prize in 1904 for his contribution made in "digestive process" in dogs, where Pavlov along with his assistants introduced edible and non-edible things to dogs to watch the production of saliva, and he found that salivation (production of saliva) is a reflexive process which occurs automatically in response to stimulus.

Pavlov further found or observed that dogs start salivating even before they are given food or smell.

After observing the behaviour or the response of the dogs when they started salivating even before the presence of food or smell, it made him think its other possible causes. Further observations and more experiments were done to find the cause. Finally, he came to know that it was the result of "learning". He found it when he paired food with ringing bell, after the food (meat powder) and ringing bell were presented together for several times, they used the bell alone. It was found that dogs were salivating to the sound of bell. This is how dogs learnt to associate bell with food which was able to trigger salivation. Hence, after making several conditioning trials and proper observations, it was concluded and believed that dogs begin to salivate after they hear the sound (metronome) which means that metronome is stimulating the saliva in dogs.

5.3.3 Social Learning Theory: The originator of social learning theory was Albert Bandura. This theory posts that learning is an outcome of interaction with each other, observation, modelling and imitation. It makes a bridge between behaviourist and cognitive theory of learning because it generated awareness/attention, memory and motivation. Most human behaviour is learnt observationally through modelling. From observing others, one forms an idea of how new behaviours are performed, and on later occasions, this coded information serves as a guide for action. There are following conditions which are effective for modelling.
1. Attention.
2. Retention.
3. Reproduction.
4. Motivation.

A. Attention: There are various factors that can influence (increase or decrease) the amount of attention paid on a particular event or activity. Those factors can be:
- Affective valence.
- Prevalence.
- Complexity of situation.

- Distinctiveness.
- Functional value.

B. Retention: It depends upon how attentively one has watched or heard something, which further leads to memorization. Paying attention on something helps in memorizing later on, when required. It may include mental images, rehearsal, coding, etc. when a person likes something a lot, he/she wants to bring it in his/her behaviour. And he/she starts learning it through memorizing images, coding etc.

For example, a person watches a movie in a theatre. He found some dialogues to be so good and he tries to learn them through images, coding, etc.

C. Reproduction: Retention helps in reproducing the image already formed or the coding done.

D. Motivation: Here, the good reason to imitate gives the motivation to recall.

5.3.4 Cognitivism Theory: The theory of cognitivism focuses on core (inner) mental processes which include the following:
- Thinking.
- Memory.
- Knowing.
- Problem solving.

This theory focuses on these processes which are being run in a human's mind. It is necessary to explore more and more to understand what is going on in a human's mind. This theory dominated over the behaviourism theory in 1960s. This theory uses mind as a computer which receives information, processes it and provides the desired results.

Cognitive psychology is concerned about the way people think, understand, know, comprehend with the outside world, within themselves and how their ways of thinking about the world influences their behaviour.

5.3.5 Gestalt Psychology: In the early 1900s, Gestalt psychology was developed in Germany. Gestalt is a German word which means form or shape, which can be understood as an organization/configuration. It emphasises on the "whole of the human experience" as they found that the perception becomes meaningful only when it is observed completely as a whole and good perception results in learning. For example, when we look at a wall made of bricks, we are looking at the whole i.e. the standing structure rather than breaking it down into different smaller bricks. Different people interpret differently based upon their past experiences. Gestalt psychologists have the opinion that in order for learning to occur, one must have the prior knowledge of the related area. They consider learning as an internal mental process which includes insight, processing information, memorizing and perception.

5.3.6 Attribution Theory: This theory works on providing an explanation to the people about the cause of happening of an event or a particular behaviour. This theory takes an assumption that people try to provide the reason of what they did. They tend to make cause and effect relationship even if there is none. People are naïve psychologists. This theory focuses on achievement. The important factors affecting this theory are ability, effort, task difficulty and luck whereas its dimensions are point of control, stability and controllability.

5.4 Learning Styles

Every learner has his own style of learning. Some of them learn best while practicing while some others learn by working in their brains with related theories and the remaining learners may prefer their own way of learning which may include verbal, visual, logical, solitary, social, physical etc.

Learning styles have been divided into different categories as mentioned below.

5.4.1 Physical Category: Those learners fall under this category, who use their physical senses to learn something:
- Visual learning style i.e. reading, watching video, demo, etc.
- Auditory learning style: Here, learners use their 'hearing'

through ears to learn the subject matter. The techniques used here may be lectures, G.D., listening to CDs, etc.
- Motor learning style: This style is also known as kinesthetic style. In this style of learning, learners prefer to practice the task by doing it physically in order to learn it. Some learners solve and learn things in their heads but in this case they prefer to do it practically. Techniques used here are practical experiments, field work, role playing, etc.

5.4.2 Cognitive Category: This category belongs to the learner's way of thinking. The previously discussed approach was physically cantered whereas cognitive approach is mentally cantered. For example, when you read or hear something, the image starts forming in your mind and it processes further analysis.

5.4.3 Affective Category: The affective category addresses the acquisition of attitudes and values. Factors affecting here are:

1. **Physiological Factors:** These factors include internal factors and external factors.
   - **Internal Factors:** These are the factors which can reduce or diminish one's learning ability e.g., hunger, illness, etc.
   - **External Factors:** These are environmental factors or environmental comforts which can affect one's learning ability, e.g., noise, temperature, level of light etc.
2. **Psychological Factors:** These are the factors affecting our emotions which can further affect our learning ability. It includes:
   - **Internal Factors:** These may include one's personal style, motivation, risk taking, willingness, etc.
   - **External Factors:** These may include stress at work, style of others, support, etc.

6

Competency Mapping

6.1 Competency Defined

In 1960, David McClelland's landmark article in American Psychologist, asserted that companies should have people based on competencies rather than just scores.

In 1973, his article brought a turning point. The article said that the traditional achievement and score of intelligence may not predict success. So, it is required to map the competencies to get a particular job done effectively.

For mapping the competencies, behaviour event interviewing (BEI) was developed by McBer. Also, in 1970s, as a result of limitations of performance appraisal, to predict the future performance, the focus was made on the areas of potential appraisal and assessment centres.

Competency is a set of skills, abilities, knowledge and personal attributes that contribute to increased employee performance.

According to Boyatzis (1982), "A capacity that exists in a person leads to behaviour that meets the job demands within the parameters of organizational environment, and that, in turn brings about the desired results".

According to Rankin (2002), "Competencies are definition of skills and behaviours that an organization expects their staff to practice in work".

According to UNIDO (2002), "A competency is a set of skills, related knowledge and attributes that allow an individual to successfully perform a task or an activity within a specific function or a job".

According to Ansfield (1997), "Competency is a set of underlying characteristics of a person that results in an effective superior performance".

According to Hayes (1979), "Competencies are generic knowledge, motive, trait, social role or a skill of a person linked to superior performance on the job".

6.2 Classification of Competencies
Competencies have been classified as follows:

6.2.1 Core Competencies: An important internal capability in an employee which is required by the organization or we can say that these competencies define what an organization values most in its employees. The concept of core competency in management theory was introduced by C.K. Prahalad and Gary Hamel.

Core competencies are required to be changing according to the change in business environment. These are flexible in nature. In a changing business environment, the circumstances change and so do the core competencies.

6.2.2 Functional/Professional Competencies: In order to achieve the optimized level of performance in an organization, these types of competencies are grouped for each job. These are classified as:
- Behavioural competencies.
- Threshold competencies (base minimum required to perform a job).
- Differentiating competencies (these competencies differentiate superior employees from average employees).

Behaviour competencies are observable and measurable. These competencies are necessary to achieve organizational goals.

Differentiating competencies differentiate superior employees from the average employees whereas threshold competencies are the base minimum competencies which are required to perform a job.

6.3 Competency Mapping
It basically encompasses identifying a set of competencies which are required to perform a given job in a given time period

which is usually done by dividing the job into activities and recognizing the competencies (which may be technical, conceptual knowledge, managerial etc. in nature) which are required to perform the job successfully. Hence, it is a process of describing the competencies which are most critical to success in a work role, based on identifying and analyzing the competencies.

Also, we can say that competency mapping is a SWOT analysis of an individual which is basically done to improve his future performance. By knowing or analyzing strengths, weaknesses, opportunities and threats, he can overcome his weaknesses and avail the opportunities available in order to perform better.

6.4 Need for Competency Mapping

In competency based system, both the employer and the employees have benefit. It makes a transparent blueprint for recruitment, performance valuation etc. with minimized level of personal judgement and subjectivity. It has been further discussed below.

For an organization:
- To attain the objectives strategically, it is needed.
- Competency mapping helps in getting best results with training and development.
- Also, it is very helpful in recruitment and selection of employees.
- In order to make performance appraisal in a systematic manner and to retain the talent, competency mapping is needed.
- It helps in improving job satisfaction level and employees' career growth.
- It supports company in making compensation plans for its employees.
- It helps in defining roles and responsibilities of the employees very clearly for managers.
- Competency mapping makes a transparent blueprint for recruitment and selection, compensation plans,

performance evaluation, training and development programs which reduces the chances of personal judgement and subjectivity.
- It helps managers in identifying the level of performance of employees.
- It creates improved level of communication.
- It develops harmony by improving employer-employee relationship.
- It helps employees by understanding their roles and responsibilities very clearly.
- Employees try to improve their competencies and accept challenges.
- It helps in providing job satisfaction among employees.
- It helps in making their career plans.
- Based on his competency, an employee knows about his compensation package.

6.5 Process of Competency Mapping

The process of competency mapping includes the following steps:

Step I: First of all, the posts are described where the need is felt to map the competencies.

Step II: Next step is to identify the location of the posts in the organization structure where competency mapping is required.

Step III: To know well, the objectives of the positions in an organization—where an opportunity exists with sufficient knowledge of role objectives—and the reason of existence of position is known and the role purpose is found out.

Step IV: Next step is to obtain a job description of position in order to make a list of different tasks to be done by an individual holding that position.

Step V: Here, the tasks which an individual expects to perform are identified.

Step VI: In this step, interview of the individual holding the position takes place regarding the actual qualities i.e. knowledge, skill, attitude required to perform the job and this process has to be repeated with all the members at the same position.

Step VII: Based on the competencies list, an analysis is done and editions are made wherever required and after that it is presented for the approval.

6.6 Iceberg Model of Competency

In Iceberg model, competencies are explained in an easier way to understand (Figure 6.1).

Figure 6.1: Iceberg Model of Competency

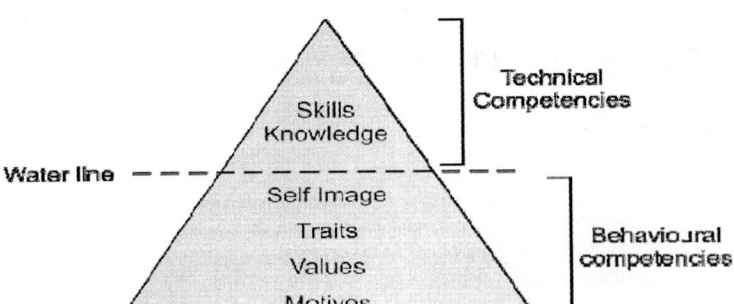

Competencies shown at the top of the iceberg are skill and knowledge. These competencies are shown above the water line which is also known as technical competencies. Being above the water line indicates that these are clearly visible and hence easy to assess. The competencies which are shown below the water line in the figure above are called behavioural competencies. These competencies are difficult to assess and much harder to develop.

Let us discuss the top visible part of the iceberg, i.e. technical competencies:

- **Skill:** Skill is the ability of a person to do something well, which can be a result of deliberate systematic and sustained effort, training or experience.
- **Knowledge:** Knowledge is the ability to use available data resources, information, skills, experience, etc. to solve

problems in related areas. For example, a company has to select an employee to work abroad (France) on a major project for a few months. The knowledge of French language by an employee can differentiate him with others and hence he can be selected, if eligible otherwise.
- **Trait:** Trait is an aspect of an employee's behaviour that explains his enduring personal characteristics.
- **Motives:** It is an underlying need that drives a person's behaviour in a specific area. Competencies vary according to the type of job.

In core competencies, collaboration competency shows how well an employee collaborates with others to attain the common mission, vision and goal, viz.:
- Willingly participating.
- Taking initiative.
- Sharing useful information.
- Expressing ideas and concerns.
- Encouraging others to give ideas.
- Engaging right people at right place while looking forward to attain goals.
- Recommending improvement wherever required based on monitoring process.
- Applying team strength in the right direction.

Problem solving competency is the competency that requires the anticipation of problem, identification and defining the same, while going in depth to find the root cause of the problem and its subsequent solution.

6.7 Tools and Techniques

For the purpose of performance appraisal of employees, traditionally there were some performance appraisal methods which had their own weaknesses.

Some of the traditional assessment methods are: ranking method, man to man comparison, group appraisal, grading, field review, critical incident method, graphic rating scale method, essay method, forced choice distribution, checklists, forced distribution, etc.

To overcome the weaknesses of traditional methods, modern tools have been introduced which are as follows.

6.7.1 Assessment Centre: There are a number of assessors to test an employee in different social situations. It is like simulation method (job related). The assessors observe an employee through different methods i.e. role play, group discussion, business games, etc. and evaluate them in individual situations as well as in group.

Here, the actual performance of the employer is compared with the standards already set by the company. If some negative deviation is found, corrective action is suggested.

6.7.2 Behaviourally-anchored Ranking Scale (BARS): BARS was originated in 1963 by P.C. Smith and L.M. Kendall. An in depth understanding of each position's main tasks is required here along with the behaviours which are expected from the individuals to perform such tasks. Then the behaviours are observed while the performance of the task is going on and then they are rated accordingly, i.e. excellent, good, fair and poor.

6.8 Management by Objectives (MBO)

MBO was proposed by Peter Drucker who suggested point participation of superiors as well as subordinates while setting the objectives to be achieved. The advantage here is that after setting the objectives jointly, an employee can do self-audit and based on that he can identify the skill/s needed by him (if any) to achieve the objective. Here, the employees monitor their own performance. For example, a sales person has to reach the goal of selling 2,000 units by November 2016. Here, by doing a self-audit, he can identify what types of additional skills are required to achieve the target (by knowing his weaknesses, he can take required actions to overcome such weaknesses).

The process of MBO has been discussed as follows:

6.8.1 Setting Individual Objectives: Here, the objectives are set by the managers jointly with the individual employee. While setting the objectives it is taken care of that the objectives being set should be specific, relevant, measurable and must be achieved within the given time period. When the objectives are set with employee participation, it helps him make plans in his own way to achieve them.

6.8.2 Providing Feedback and Performance Evaluation: Managers and employees review the progress. The employee comes to know of the success or failure. It helps him understand the deviation and the reasons for those deviations.

6.8.3 Giving Rewards: After achieving the objectives, employees should be rewarded for their performance. Rewards may include promotion, recognition, increase in salary, etc.

6.8.4 360° Feedback: In a 360° assessment tool, any party involved with the rating, rates an employee. Hence, in this method, the ratee (employee being rated) gets rated by everyone involved e.g. supervisor, peers, subordinates, himself, customers etc.

6.9 Effects of Competency Mapping on Other HRD Systems

The effect of competency mapping on other HRD systems has been explained below.

6.9.1 Recruitment and Selection: The approach of competency mapping saves time and money of an organization. Also it provides an organization, the expert staff.

It benefits the organization as now the organization knows the skill set/competencies required. Also, the right person now has the right place/job which ensures a good fit between a skilled person and his suitable place.

Providing an expert at the right place helps an organization to increase its productivity and growth. Also by appointing the right person at the right place provides satisfaction to him. Most important thing that has been noted here in competency mapping is that the skills of an individual are matched with the job requirements.

6.9.2 Performance Management System: In performance

management system, competency mapping helps the system by making the employees analyze the feedback provided to them regarding the type of work assigned to them and what has been performed by them and how it has been performed.

In a nutshell, it helps employer to know the gap between expected performance and enhanced competencies. Also, it provides the standards for the appraisal. The training which has already been provided to an employee, competency mapping supporting performance management system helps an employee to know what he/she has achieved after training by evaluation of on job performance.

6.9.3 Training: In training, competency mapping helps to know in advance the expectations from an individual at the work place not only theoretically but also practically.

Nowadays, in a rapidly changing technological business environment, the knowledge in wider aspect is required so that it can make an employee compatible to work in changing situations. In this scenario, his ability to transfer and apply skills, attitude and knowledge in respective areas as demanded by the business is also required.

In this way, competency mapping helps employees and the organization in betterment of their future.

Employees, besides getting competencies also get much confident about what they are doing and what they are supposed to do in the changing circumstances. Besides handling issues in a changing business environment, it also helps in building self-confidence which further develops employees' interest which readies them for any future challenges.

This also motivates them as it helps in increasing their knowledge and development of their skills which further contributes to transfer of knowledge, attitude, etc.

6.9.4 Compensation Management: Employees demand an increased package of salary for their added knowledge to work in the current business environment. To meet their demand, they are offered lucrative packages as per their competencies which are now enhanced as compared to the earlier ones.

Nowadays, employees are working on enhancing their competencies, not only to get more salary as compared to what they were getting earlier but also for their survival in a challenging business world.

Accepting new challenges day by day in today's business world and by enhancing their competencies makes them confident enough to get competency based pay structure which further encourages them to gain more knowledge so that they can accept further challenges.

7
Socialization and Orientation of Employees

To retain talented employees in an organization has become a challenge these days especially when they are new. Researchers have found that during the first few months on job, maximum attrition occurs which is a cause of concern. To overcome this problem, greater focus is given to help new employees in understanding the corporate culture, developing team work between new comers and the existing staff members, making them feel comfortable so that they can become familiar on social as well as professional level and a strong bond can be developed which would help in increasing productivity and reducing the employee turnover. This is called *employees' socialization*.

7.1 Organizational Socialization

Organizational socialization takes place whenever an employee crosses an organizational boundary, whether this is external (i.e. between organizations) or internal (e.g. functional or hierarchical).

Organizational socialization can include changes in or the development of new skills, knowledge, abilities, attitudes, values and relationships, and the development of appropriate sense-making frameworks.

The newcomer's characteristics and tactics and organization's efforts help in making adjustments into the new business environment in gaining a clear and strong understanding of his own role in the organization for the position assigned to him and also it helps him in understanding the organizational culture (Table 7.1).

7.2 Socialization Process

The process of socialization includes the following phases:

7.2.1 Anticipatory Socialization: This is the stage which occurs before joining the organization, when the potential employee talks to the organization's recruiters, managers, etc.; the expectations' state taking place in the minds of (new hires/potential employee) about their job and the organization. To know the values and norms before joining an organization or any type of work that one is going to start in near future is always helpful.

Hence, it helps in easing the group entry and once they enter the organization, it further helps them by making competent interaction.

Table 7.1: Organizational Socialization for Newcomers and Managers

For Newcomers	For Managers
Gain sufficient information about organization whether it is formal or informal	Monitor each newcomer very closely
How much own culture is to be set aside to adopt culture of the organization	Based on observation, determine the best approach to help newcomers in adopting the culture of the organization
Making a decision about how much degree of loyalty is to be given to the organization	Provide relevant and required information the newcomers need about the organization and help them solve difficulties and issues, if any

For example, medical science students learning how to behave like doctors/pharmacists or when students of law learn how to behave like lawyers, it helps them to know in advance the norms and the values in an organization or the profession which they are going to join.

7.2.2 Organizational Encounter: On joining a new job, employees get training. Here, the managers help their employees to understand their duties and roles. Also, managers try to understand the stress level a newcomer is facing and hence they help them by overcoming such issues and difficulties.

It is expected to have a clear and complete understanding of the organization as well as roles to be performed.

7.2.3 Settling in/Metamorphosis: After encounter phase, this stage comes when newcomers start feeling comfortable with their jobs and they become socialized now.

7.3 Learning in Socialization

Socialization is a process of learning as the newcomers start learning from the very first day, they join the organization. Generally also, we learn different things throughout our life. Now coming back to socialization in an organization, the newcomers learn a lot and based on the experiences, their attitudes and behaviours are formed.

At the stage of preliminary learning, a newcomer thinks about what he needs to learn and why is the learning required? After getting sufficiently convinced by the reasons to learn, he finds the source of learning i.e. from where he can get fully equipped with the information/learning material which is required.

After preliminary learning, he wants to learn about the organization. Learning about the organization includes organizational goals, values, policies etc.

Now since the newcomer has the knowledge about the organization, it is time to learn how to function in a group. Learning in a group requires making friends who can teach different things and give suggestions in their area of expertise.

Then he needs to learn how to perform the job assigned. For this, he needs the skill set and knowledge related to that specific area. In personal learning category, the newcomer tries to make a self-image and finds different ways to feel self-motivated.

7.4 Socialization Categories

Organizational socialization categories can be divided into following parts:

7.4.1 Formal vs. Informal Strategy: In formal strategy of socialization, a formal training program is conducted to socialize the new employees whereas in case when informal strategy is adopted, no training is provided for socializing of the employees. They learn by themselves in an informal environment. This is done at the regular working environment where newcomers come in contact with the existing employees i.e. colleagues and others. Hence, they come to know about the organization culture informally.

7.4.2 Individual vs. Collective Strategy: Socialization programs when conducted on one to one basis, is termed as an individual strategy. Here, in individual strategy, a supervisor is assigned to teach the organizational culture to the newcomer and on the other hand, in collective strategy, a group of newcomers are educated at once. Collective strategy is less expensive and less time consuming as compared to individual strategy.

7.4.3 Fixed vs. Variable Strategy: While implementing fixed strategy of socialization, time and duration of each and every activity is planned and pre-determined. A schedule is made which is required to be followed whereas in case of variable strategy there is no pre-determined or planned schedule to be followed. It depends upon the convenience of the parties.

7.4.4 Sequential vs. Non-sequential Strategy: When it is required by the organization to complete a specific level during the socialization program before entering the next level/position, it is called sequential strategy as it follows the sequence to move on to the next stage whereas in case of non-sequential strategy, there is no requirement to complete a specific stage to move on to the next position.

7.4.5 Serial vs. Disjunctive Strategy: Before placing newcomers to their designated positions, experienced superiors are required to conduct a socialization program for them. This strategy is called serial strategy.

In disjunctive strategy, there is no such requirement to

attend the socialization programme.

7.4.6 Tournament vs. Contest-oriented Strategy: On the basis of an employee's skill set and educational qualifications, different groups are formed and each group is provided different socialization program whereas in case of contest-oriented strategy, no such groups are formed.

7.4.7 Investiture vs. Divestiture Strategy: These types of strategies are based upon the compatibility between newcomer's culture and the organizational culture. When compatibility is found between newcomer's culture and the organizational culture, values and beliefs which are brought in the organization by the newcomer's are reinforced. This type of socialization strategy is called investiture. Divestiture strategy on the other hand exists when no compatibility is found between the newcomer's and organizational culture and attempts are made to modify or nullify the culture brought in by the newcomer. This type of strategy is called divestiture.

7.5 Consequences of Socialization

The consequences of socialization can be positive as well as negative. These have been discussed as follows:

7.5.1 Positive Consequences: If the socialization is provided to the employees in the required and proper manner, it results in bringing job satisfaction, sense of cooperation and belongingness, motivation, productivity and hence emotional commitment to the organization.

Positive consequences are the result of successful socialization which is good for an employee as well as the organization.

7.5.2 Negative Consequences: Negative consequences are the result of unsuccessful socialization. It can be due to:
- **Insufficient Level:** Insufficient level of socialization results in dissatisfaction, poor performance at job, behaviour that is unacceptable, violation of rules and regulations which can further can to employee turnover.
- **Too High Level:** Too high level of socialization is also

not required as it results in lack of creativity, dogmatic thinking, etc.

Hence, planning an effective socialization plan is an important step to be taken before starting the socialization and for that very purpose, the managers themselves should know the cultural values of their organization.

7.6 Orientation of New Employees

Induction or orientation is a technique by which a new employee is rehabilitated into the changed surroundings and introduced to the practices, policies and purposes of the organization.

Introduction of new employees to the work environment which consists of the job itself, co-workers and organization in a planned way to familiarize them to the situation or environment is known as orientation. The orientation program helps in reducing the stress that new employees feel while joining a new job.

A new employee faces new rules, new co-workers, new bosses, new work environment and responsibilities. All these things bring a feeling of insecurity and anxiety in him which is required to be removed. The feeling of insecurity and anxiety in him does not let him feel comfortable in the working environment and it may lead to increased percentage of employee turnover at the end of the year. The retention of good and talented employees is always required in an organization and for that very purpose, we need to make them feel comfortable first.

Employees' orientation has the following objectives:
- To convey the goals of the company. It is important for the newcomers to know about the objectives of the company which is the main reason of its existence. The knowledge about company's rules and procedures help employees, work in the new environment.
- To tell them about the history of the company, benefits, etc. It is done so that employees can learn about the

organizational culture (e.g. how things are done in the company i.e. methods, acceptable behaviour, etc.).
- It is an opportunity for the CEO to welcome newcomers and interact with them. In this way, he can have direct communication with the newcomers.
- It provides information to employees regarding benefits and other matters. Also, it provides help to the employees by providing them training, career guidance etc.

New employees who enter the organization have a lot going on in their minds. They have a lot of questions to ask and they eagerly wait for the answers. Hence, these questions are required to be answered effectively and at the right time. The possible questions can be:
- Organization's mission?
- Organisation exists for?
- What are my rights and duties?
- What is my role in the organization?
- What is my authority and responsibility?
- What are the performance standards?
- How can I fit in the organization and with co-workers etc.?
- How to make good relationships here?
- What type of training they are going to provide us?
- What can be the objectives of training and when will they provide it?
- What is my future in the organization?

Hence, the orientation program must be properly designed to deliver the necessary information and to answer the questions which employees have in their minds.

In order to provide right answers to the questions that new employees can ask, the manager who has been assigned for the orientation program must be fully equipped with all the information required which can be usually divided in the following two phases.

7.6.1 First Phase: The general introduction of the company and cultural aspects are generally combined together in the first phase of orientation program. The person who is suitable to present the information is selected for the orientation program. He is expected to be fully equipped with all the information needed to be delivered e.g. the company's mission statement, company standards, policies/procedures, company's expectations, management tradition, management philosophies and strategic beliefs, acceptable norms, personnel information, insurance, benefits, etc.

All the above mentioned information should be available so that the questions raised by the newcomers can be answered right on time.

7.6.2 Second Phase: After the company's general information phase of orientation program, here comes the second phase of specific job orientation which focuses on job performance. Here, the employees are informed about job responsibilities as described in the job description, details about equipment needed for the performance of job and their location, working environment and working conditions.

On a tour to the departmental property, newcomers are introduced to every important thing and the other employees working in the department. Also, they are told about the work timings, break time, dining, payroll, etc.

Employees are interested in their growth opportunities in the company or knowing about their scope in the company. In orientation program, they are told about the growth and developmental opportunities that they have or they will be having in the future.

After gaining all the information which is job related, they now have an idea of working, the technology which is being used in the organization and the knowledge of complete working environment. It makes them feel comfortable when they start working.

A successful orientation program leads to reduction in employee turnover. Also, it helps in reducing anxiety and nervousness which employees face in the first few days of joining a new job.

7.7 Difference between Socialization and Orientation

Table 7.2 provides points of difference between socialization and orientation.

Table 7.2: Socialization and Orientation

Basis	Socialization	Orientation
Type	Socialization is an informal process of learning about the culture of the organization by the newcomer	It is a formal process of learning about the organization by the newcomer
Term	Socialization is a long-term process	Orientation is a short-term process
Aim	The objective here is to introduce the newcomer to the culture of an organization including attitudes, values, beliefs, etc.; basically, including work environment in depth	The objective of orientation programme is to introduce the newcomer to the organization to help removing his anxiety and nervousness on joining a new company
Frequency	Socialization is a continuous process as employees keep learning about organization throughout their career	Orientation is usually a one-time activity which is conducted when a new employee starts a job/career in the organization

8
Training and Development

Corporate change takes place when adjustments are required to be made in a company's environment. Based on the needs for changes required, the process begins with identifying training, education and development needs.

A few questions must be well-known in advance in case of a corporate change:
- What is the need for training?
- What purpose is going to be fulfilled/accomplished by the efforts of HRD?

Based on the answers, it depends upon the management to select the type of suitable methods to solve the problem. Nature of HRD objectives are kept in mind well before deciding about the particular method selection.

8.1 Training Defined

"Training is a systematic development of the knowledge, skills and attitudes required by an individual to perform adequately a given task or job"—*Michael Armstrong*.

"Training is the act of increasing knowledge and skills of an employee for doing a particular job"—*Edwin B. Flippo*.

"Training is a planned process to modify attitude, knowledge or skill behaviour through a learning experience to achieve effective performance in any activity or range of activities. Its purpose, in the work situation is to develop the abilities of the individual and to satisfy current and future manpower needs of the organization"—*Manpower Services Commission, U.K.*

8.2 Importance of Training and Development

It is always necessary to equip individuals with the skills which are required to function fully in an organization. Hence, in order to maintain skilled and talented human resources in an organization, it is important to provide them training and development opportunities. It would help in the development of both employees as well as the organization.

With the introduction of *new technology* into the business, employees need to be trained. But these days, training has become a challenge due to increasing competition, advancement in technologies and globalization.

8.2.1 Product or Service Quality: With so many competitors available in the market, companies want to differentiate their product from others and for that purpose they are increasingly focusing on the quality of product or service. To meet up to the expected level of quality, human resources need to be fully trained. Employees must have the skills to perform their duties—problem solving skills and skills which are required to correct faults.

8.2.2 New Technology: The introduction of new technology in the market and the demand for labour that possesses the required knowledge and skills has increased. Companies cannot take the advantage of latest technology if its human resources do not possess the skills required to use the latest technology.

8.2.3 Flexibility: In the rapidly changing business environment, the employees of an organization are required to adapt to the changing environment. Only then, an organization will be able to move with the flow in order to survive successfully. In this scenario, employees should be willing to learn new skills and hence flexible in doing different job tasks. This means that employees need to be multi-skilled.

One of the main challenges here is that some employees who are working in an organization, are resistant to change. If employees are not willing to change or learn, they cannot be flexible. In this case, the first step to be taken should be to train them to accept the change and learn different things.

8.2.4 Committed Employees: There is an increasing realization that the graduate recruits are willing to work in companies which provide opportunities to learn new skills and grow. Such recruits do not join companies which do not provide their employees the opportunities to learn new skills. The companies can invest in such type of employees who are willing to learn following the change.

8.2.5 Some Managers Follow Cascade Training: In this scenario, a company sends only one worker for training and expects him to train others in his team. Here, in this case, companies can take the advantage by spending less money on training (training cost of one employee vs. training cost of the whole team). Hence, if one worker is trained, the whole team gets trained provided the trained worker has fully understood the concept otherwise the whole team will suffer.

8.3 HRD Process

The HRD process undertakes the following steps:

8.3.1 Determining the HRD Needs: The first step in HRD process is to determine the need for providing training and development to the employees' i.e. what is expected from the employees or what type of change (in terms of addition in their knowledge/skills) is expected from them?

HRD needs can arise due to legislature issue (change in policies) and lack of performance (performance not up to mark or as per standards). Introduction of new technology and methods can be one of the causes.

Emergence of new products/services in the market requires the need of adequately train human resources. Higher standards of performance can be another cause.

It can be done by doing the following types of analysis:
- Organisational analysis.
- Task analysis.
- Personal analysis.

A. Organizational Analysis: While conducting organisational analysis, the needs for providing training and development programme is identified and recognized everywhere in the organization keeping in mind the objectives of the organization.

Organizational analysis can be done by identifying the existing knowledge, skills and abilities of the employees as well as future requirements of their knowledge, skills and abilities in performing future jobs taking into consideration the internal and external factors.

The departments or areas in the organization, where there is high turnover, low or poor performance, rate of observation is high or has an increasing trend are also kept in mind while doing this analysis.

A close observation is done to recognize the performance of employees (how they are performing the tasks, methods of doing work etc.) and their complaints are well noted to identify the type of problems occurring and the frequency of same type of complaint or different complaints, to find the reason of complaint, to know whether it is due to technical issue or due to lack knowledge in an employee(s) or there is some other cause.

The *frequency of accidents* occurring in an organization during the operations shows that there is something wrong. It has to be found here that whether it is due to lack of skill amongst the labour handling the machines or is it the inappropriate method that is being used.

Exit interviews help the organization in knowing the performance as well as the weaknesses which help in providing improvement by helping in decision-making about the type of training required to control the situation.

Also, the *types of tools or equipments* which are being used while performing the job are closely observed to know the type of technology being used. Due to increase in competition among the industries domestically as well as globally, it has become important to use the latest technological methods to face the competition and survive in the market. If old (manual) methods are still in use, it needs to be changed and for that purpose, training of employees is required.

B. Task Analysis: While conducting task analysis, following two factors should be considered:

The relevance of task and behaviour comes under the factor *importance*. The other main and important factor to be considered is *proficiency* of the employees. It means the competence of employees in performing a task assigned to them.

The proficiency of the employees can be measured by surveys, performance appraisal etc.

To do a task analysis, job description and job specification are taken into consideration as they provide useful and required information about the type of performance expected from the employees and the type of skills necessary to perform the job. The gap (if any), helps in deciding the training needs.

C. Personal Analysis: Personal analysis is the next analysis which is made to determine the needs of human resource development. In this type of analysis, an answer is required for the following questions:
1. Which employee/employees need to be trained?
2. What type of training is required?

To get the answers to these questions, different tests, role playing methods and assessment centres can be helpful.

Thereafter, employees' performance is checked whether it meets the standards or not. If there is some gap in actual performance and performance as per the standards, he required area of training is analyzed in which they need training.

There are a few other methods to identify the training needs of an employee which are elaborated below.

8.3.2 Determining Training Priorities: Because training requires a lot of budget, it has to be done keeping in mind the objectives of the company, time, cost, ability and motivation of the trainer. In case of limited budget, the priority areas to improve the health of the organization are considered first to get results which are visible in a short span of time.

8.3.3 Setting Training Objectives: Based on the training priorities, the objectives of training are set. These objectives of training can be set in all the areas where training need is determined. These objectives should be set in measurable terms so that it may be easy to compare the expected results with the results obtained in order to find whether the training objectives are fully met or not.

The training objectives can be set as follows:

1. **Based on Work Quantity:** In this case, the standards or objectives are set in terms of quantity e.g. to a salesman, to sell 20 units of a product in a month can be set as a target.
2. **Based on Work Quality:** Quality can be measured in the form of less waste/errors, reduced cost of production, etc. For example, if the production is made with less waste and less cost of production (comparatively) in a given time period, it can be said that the quality of production has improved.
3. **Based on Time:** Training objective can be set by taking into consideration the time factor. For example, the work is accomplished or the standards are met within the given period of time or lesser time.

8.3.4 Selecting the HRD Method: Based on the training needs, the most appropriate method(s) are selected to train the employees to get the desired results. Different methods of training have been discussed as follows. These methods include training methods for employees (operative), managers and entry level professionals.

A. Coaching/Mentoring: Coaching is a method of training in which an opportunity is given to the manager to teach/train an employee. In this case, the subordinate, who is under study is also given the opportunity to observe the problem or situation to perform specific business tasks and make decisions. Based on that, the manager or the coach is expected to have thorough knowledge of the job and the objectives of the organization. In some organizations, a post *"assistant to"* is created for this purpose.

B. Business Games: Simulations based on actual situations in the business are put in front of the employees' participating. They are assigned different roles like marketing manager, controller etc. and a problem is put in front of them to solve, keeping in mind the different roles/positions assigned to them. After they provide the decision, it is seen to what extent the problem is solved based on a computer program simulating the real business problem.

C. Case Study: In this method of training, trainees are given the same type of business problems to solve based on the detailed information provided to them.

Trainees are expected to provide a solution to the given problem considering an actual business scenario.

D. Conference Method: The professionals/employees of same interest are gathered here to discuss issues on the related topic. Discussing the issues here brings more ideas from the minds of different professionals. The group leader takes the charge of making the discussion to the point, if it goes out of the area assigned. It helps in solving actual problems being faced by them in daily routine.

E. Behaviour Modelling: In this method of training, the demonstration/video tapes are played in front of employees so that they can understand and interpret the decision made by the models in real business problems. This method of training is being used today to train the supervisor while making performance appraisals to correct the performance which is not as per the standards already set and improving safety habits while handling different complaints. It also helps supervisor when he is working as a mediator in various conflicting groups.

This model of training helps the supervisor in solving various problems by getting different ideas and interpretation. He relates the problem (already demonstrated) with the real problem and tries to solve it in the same manner (after getting ideas from the demo).

F. In Basket Training: Here, the participants are given information such as memoranda, reports etc. ranging from urgent to non-urgent but these are in no order and the participant is supposed to take action based on his decision-making ability.

G. Internships: In this method of training, the students who are studying in the universities work as interns in an organization related to their ongoing study area. Here, they practically perform their study related job in the organization. It helps them to gain the practical knowledge of theoretical learning/studies. Also, it helps them knowing whether practically doing that specific job appeals to them or not.

H. Role Playing: It is one of the management development techniques where participants are expected to solve or respond to the particular problem while doing it. Here, they learn to handle different issues by doing them practically.

Also in some cases, the participants are assigned different roles to solve a given problem. Keeping in mind the roles, participants are expected to respond to the problem.

I. Job Rotation: In this method, employees are moved to different types of job so that they can gain knowledge in different areas. It adds to their knowledge by doing different types of work.

J. Programmed Instruction: Here, the trainee is given information which is divided in different parts. He reads the information already divided in the sequence and after reading and understanding it, he is expected to respond to certain questions. Then he gives the response and if his response is correct, based on the feedback which is available in the program, he proceeds to the next level and he repeats the previous level if the response is incorrect.

K. Classroom Lecture: In this method, a lecturer delivers the lecture to a number of employees taking part in the training. The lecturer teaches a number of employees at the same time. It is more effective if the number of participants is less. He uses audio visuals to make teaching effective.

L. On the Job Training: This method of training is an informal method which allows the employees to ask their problems while performing the assigned tasks. The manager here is expected to provide the appropriate solution to the employees learning under this method.

M. Apprenticeship Training: This is a traditional method of providing training usually to the employees engaged in craft jobs i.e. plumber, carpenter, etc. Here, the trainees are paid some amount of money also.

N. Vestibule Training: In this method, employees are provided training away from their area of job. Here, they are given the equipments which are going to be same in the actual work area. This improves the skill set of employees in the related area of job.

8.3.5 Selecting HRD Media: There are different media which can be used while training the employees. The appropriate media is required to be selected for the training purpose.

The different types of media being used these days are as follows:

1. **Computer Assisted Instruction (CAI):** In this media of training, which is a new technique, trainees interact with the computer to learn. They are provided instructional material. CAI programs use tutorials, drill and practice, simulation and problem solving approaches and then they also test their understanding.
2. **Distance Learning:** This is the new concept already introduced in developed countries where two-way interaction is done using television. Here, a trainer can respond to the class anywhere in the world.
3. **Audio-visual Aids:** These include use of films, video tapes, audio tapes, CCTV, video teleconferencing, etc.
- **Audio Tapes and Videos:** These are being commonly used to train the employees these days. These have an important feature of replay whenever required by the trainees to learn.
- **Films:** Films are a combination of colour, music, motion and much more elements and these are very commonly used as a training media.
- **Overhead Projector (OHP):** Traditional method works by passing lights through transparency to make image on the screen. These days, it is used for colourful visual presentations.

- **Flip Charts/Slap Boards**: Traditional method as well as inexpensive one, helps the trainer to put focus on major points and elaborate them.

8.4 Implementing HRD Programme

Implementing HRD programme is difficult as it requires convincing the participants about the advantages of the program. Keeping in mind the objectives of training program, most difficulties arise due to the following reasons:

1. Employees resist changing. They are of the opinion that training is going to bring change in their method of doing work and hence they resist it.
2. HRD managers are of the opinion that they already are too busy to implement the training program.
3. Well qualified trainer is needed who can train the employees according to the training objectives.
4. Keeping and maintaining the records of training is another problem. A record has to be maintained about the training provided and progress of employees after getting training.

Hence, to implement the training program is the most difficult task. It cannot be done unless the top managers are willing to cooperate well with the system and employees are ready to cooperate.

8.5 Evaluation of Training Programme

To evaluate the training program, expected results are compared with the actual results. There are different levels of evaluation:

- **Reaction of Trainees:** Reaction of trainees is evaluated by taking their interviews or by questionnaires. It shows whether they liked the training or not and if yes then to what extent.
- **What Did They Learn:** Here 'What did the trainees learnt' is measured by giving tests after providing them training. The tests can be given to them before providing them training and even after providing training. In this way, it becomes easier to evaluate the results by making

the comparison of their scores in the pre-training and post-training tests. If in the test, it is found that trainees have learning problem the trainer is advised to redesign the training program and provide training again.
- **Behaviour of Trainees:** By taking interviews of trainees, their behaviour is judged and how it influenced their job performance, is seen. However, to measure change in behaviour is very difficult.
- **Results Achieved:** Effect of training on achieving organizational objectives is measured by measuring productivity, sales, quality, cost of production, time factor, etc. Comparison can be made by recording pre- and post-training figures.

8.6 Problems in Training

The factors that deteriorate the quality of training program affects an organization overall. These problems have been discussed as follows:
- **No Corporate Commitment:** There are many organizations which do not want to spend money required on training of workers. They hardly spend money for training of managerial personnel which degrades the quality.
- **High training Costs:** In cases where the organizations are not financially that sound, they face the problem of high cost and infrastructure requirements for providing training.
- **Fear of Competitors:** Some organizations avoid training due to the fear of their competitors that after getting trained, the talented and well-trained employees can get attracted by higher packages by their competitors. Being an expensive programme, training employees becomes a fear for the organization as every organization wants to retain the well trained and talented employees in the organization itself.
- **Employees with Inadequate Skills:** In some cases when employees enter the organization, they do not have the

adequate skill set and to train them becomes very difficult because they need to be trained from the scratch (basic level).

9

Organizational Culture and Organizational Health

9.1 Organizational Culture Defined

There are some beliefs, values and assumptions which are shared by the people working in an organization. These values, beliefs and assumptions are reflected in their behaviour which is known as *culture* of that organization or personality of that organization.

This is the culture which is generally passed by the senior members of an organization to the new members who are joining the organization which also provides the guidelines to the employees regarding doing their work in an appropriate manner. The organizational culture also defines the boundaries for the employees (which is the restricted area).

According to Ouchi (1981), organization culture is the shared values, beliefs and behavioural norms in an organization. So, according to this, an organizational culture comprises of the following:

- Shared values (describes important things).
- Beliefs (that our thinking is true).
- Behavioural norms (how things are done here/ways of doing different things in the organization).

Some important definitions of organizational culture are as under;

"Organizational culture refers to the pattern of beliefs, values and learned ways of coping with experience that have developed during the course of an organization's history, and which tend to be manifested in its material arrangements and in the behaviour of its members"—*Andrew Brown.*

"A pattern of shared basic assumptions that a group learns

as it solves its problems of external adaptation and internal integration that has worked well enough to be considered valid and therefore, to be taught to new members as the correct ways to perceive, think and feel in relation to those problems"—*Schein*.

"The pattern of shared beliefs and values that gives members of an institution meaning, and provide them with the rules for their behaviour in the organization"—*Davis*.

Values, beliefs, norms ingrained in rituals, traditions, organization history contribute to the formation of organization culture. These elements are passed to the coming generations in the organization.

Organization culture forms an atmosphere which is generally seen or felt by its group members. This atmosphere is known as 'climate'. In other words, the elements of an organization culture i.e. shared values, beliefs and assumptions which are reflected in the perception of the people is called *organization climate*.

When a newcomer joins a job, he is told the way things are done in that organization. This is the information received through informal sources of the organization but this information contributes to the organization culture.

Likewise, every employee working in the organization has some kind of perception about the organization while working under a superior's guidance and following the policies of an organization.

Different employees working in the same organization may have different perceptions about the organization which affects their level of job satisfaction and their work quality.

The type of perception that employees have can be positive or negative. Employees having negative perception are usually dissatisfied in the organization in one way or other. And because of their dissatisfaction, they may want to leave the organization and may be searching for a new job in another organization with a hope to find the organizational culture that suits them.

9.2 Importance of Organizational Culture

A strong organizational culture is required in every organization. It helps in increasing productivity, retaining talent in the organization and hence making it successful. Its importance has been discussed as follows:

- **Engages People**: Employees engaged in work perform better. Concentrating on work results for better performance, increase in productivity and hence the increase in company's profitability.
- **Retains Talent**: Strong organizational culture helps in retaining talent in an organization. The talented employees want to work with full dedication in a strong organizational culture. If the culture is not strong enough they start looking for other jobs in the market. Gone are the days when talented employees used to work for good salary and other benefits. Now they need a lot more, important one being culture.
- **Strong Culture Changes the Meaning of Work:** Where there is a strong organization culture it helps in removing the negativity in the mind of employees about doing work; rather they feel more energetic while doing work.
- **Attracts Talent from Outside**: When a strong culture exists in an organization, talented people from outside want to join, which makes a company's image more attractive to even outsiders. Also it is beneficial for the employees to work in such an energetic working environment.
- **Success for Everyone:** Working in a strong organizational culture contributes to everyone's success.

9.3 Types of Organizational Cultures

It is important for the managements these days to know the type of culture that they are already having and the type they wish to have in order to be successful. A lot of researches have been done in this area. Based on those researches, most of the researchers or the organizational behaviourists are in the favour of having a participative and open kind of culture instead of a closed and autocratic kind.

9.3.1 Participative and Open Organizational Culture: In this type of organizational culture, workers participate in management through open communication system. No strict orders are given here but often after listening to the workers/ employees, management makes the decision. Also, more emphasis is given on team work here which results in attaining better results.

9.3.2 Autocratic and Closed Organizational Culture: In case of autocratic and closed culture, business goals are imposed or declared by autocratic leaders.

Following can be the features of an autocratic/closed organizational culture:
- Goals are imposed on employees.
- Autocratic leaders (strict rigidity).
- Strict chain of command.
- Strict accountability.
- More stress is there on the individuals instead of team work.

Hence, in a closed type of culture, goals to achieve are usually imposed on employees by autocrats. They work by using more threats and making the system stricter. The strictness is the result of existing chain of command in the organization. In such type of organizational culture, greater stress is there on employees. Here, the employees do the things, they are told or in other words they just follow the orders of their leaders.

9.4 Factors Determining an Organizational Culture

Perception of employees about the organization where they work can be determined by various factors. The main factors affecting an organization's culture have been discussed below.

9.4.1 Communication: Communication is the way to create mutual understanding by exchanging information, ideas, news etc. An organization cannot survive or operate without communication. Hence, communication should be effective i.e. right message should be communicated to the right person at right time and the recipient of the information should understand its meaning in the same way in which it was expressed. Communicating effectively helps an organization to accomplish its goals in a smoother way.

Nowadays in companies, there is a department working on refining communication to make the communication effective which is important to achieve the desired goals. The employees who are learning to make their communication effective are benefiting the company as well as themselves.

9.4.2 Motivation: Employees who have been motivated will perform better as they want to be more productive. It helps them as well as their managers. Managers motivate their employees continuously to be more effective and productive by timely rewarding them; treating them fairly and making them believe that they are important for the organization. This type of feeling brings a sense of belongingness among the employees e.g. many organizations motivate employees by giving recognition to them by selecting "employee of the week or month" based on an employee's performance etc. Many managers motivate their employees by increasing their salary, providing job security and good working conditions.

It is the task of a manager to understand the environment or the factors that help employees to work better with positive energy flowing inside the organization. Also, it helps in understanding what type of organization culture is there in the organization. A positive organization culture results in better productivity and will be seen in employees' performance.

However, there are two types of motivations which are commonly used:
1. Financial motivation.
- Cash prizes.
- Rise in wages/salary.
- Free vouchers for vacations.
2. Non-financial motivation.

- Training.
- Seminars/conferences.
- Better position.
- Involvement in decision-making.

9.4.3 Leadership: The job of a leader is to influence his subordinates to get the work done in the manner which is desired. Every leader persuades his subordinates in a different way. Thus, different leaders follow different types of leadership styles:

- **Autocratic Leadership Style:** In this type of leadership style, a leader has overall control and he very rarely takes any input from his subordinates. He makes all the decisions. He has the authority to watch closely the way of doing work by his subordinates as there is very less margin of error. This type of leadership style is generally suitable in military, construction etc.
- **Democratic Leadership Style:** This type of leadership style is very open in nature. Ideas are welcomed easily and are discussed. Everyone can participate in the discussion. People here are encouraged to share the ideas and then the best decision is made based on the overall discussion. Democratic leadership style is suitable in industry where creativity is required such as the advertising industry.
- **Laissez Faire:** Also known as non-authoritative, the leadership style here believes that people do their best when they are left alone to perform their duties after telling them their responsibilities. Laissez faire leadership style is also known as "hands off" leadership style because leaders here, provide very little or no direction to their followers.

9.5 Organizational Characteristics

One of the main factors affecting an organization's culture is the organizational characteristics. Different organizations have different sizes and level of complexities. These things vary in large organizations and small organizations. Thus, large organizations have more specializations as compared to smaller ones and also large organizations are less personal as compared to the smaller ones. In small organizations, the unions find it more difficult to organize as compared to larger ones because in case of small organizations, they find more of informal type of relationship that exists between employees and management. The specialists already working in large organizations generally can change the usual way to solve a particular problem depending upon its sensitivity.

Different type of workers working in an organization has different types of perception about the organization (atmosphere) where they work. Some people have positive views while others may have negative which contributes to the organization climate.

Administration can change or maintain the norms that an organization is already having by taking different steps. For example, hiring new employees or firing the old ones.

External environment is often helpful in changing an organization's culture by adapting new methods from outside the organization which an administrator thinks to be helpful in bringing a positive change in the organization's climate.

Change in organizational design can help in changing an organization's climate.

9.6 Organizational Health

In a rapidly changing business environment and increasing competition, an organization is expected to perform better in a way that leads to shaping a better future which is a result of continuous learning, ability to face challenges and flexibility. Hence, the ability of an organization to achieve its goals in the environment seeking improvement in organizational performance and supporting employee well-being is known as organizational health.

So, organizational health includes two main factors:
- Organizational performance.
- Employees' well-being.

Organizational performance relates to achievement of

organizational goals, targets etc.

Employees' well-being includes employee satisfaction and employees' health (social, mental and physical). Here, attention should be paid towards employee satisfaction levels because it is necessary to retain the competent employees in the organization. If the employees are not satisfied with their compensation plans, pay structure, other benefits, working conditions or the work itself, it contributes to unhealthy organization. This can be found by doing surveys. There should be a positive climate in an organization as it brings in motivation among the employees working in the organization which may further lead to dedication towards the work and hence employee retention. As far as employee's well-being is concerned, the risks related to it must be controlled. Developing risk management systems can help control the risks associated with employees' well-being.

9.6.1 Social Well-being: To reduce the risks relating to employees' social well-being, no discrimination should be encouraged among employees.

9.6.2 Physical Well-being: To improve the physical health of the employees, employee wellness programs should be started. Employees' exposure to environmental hazards while at work should be identified and properly assessed and steps must be taken to minimize those hazards. Also, employees' health hazards should be taken care of by taking steps to prevent diseases and improving their lifestyle.

9.6.3 Mental Well-being: Introducing emotional and cognitive development programs can help reduce the risk associated with employees' mental well-being. Health of an organization propels its performance. Hence, to attain higher levels of performance, an organization needs to be healthy enough.

10

Size and Characteristics of India's Human Resources

10.1 Size and Growth of Population

India's population has increased rapidly since Independence in 1947. The population increased from 36.1 crore in 1951 to 43.9 crore in 1961, to 54.8 crore in 1971, and to 68.5 crore in 1981. The census of 1991 enumerated the population at 84.4 crore which rose to 102.9 crore in 2001 and was estimated at 121 crore in 2011. Thus, after China it is India that has crossed the 1 billion (100 crore) population mark. According to a recent United Nations publication, India's population is projected to peak at 1.718 billion (171 crore) in 2060. At its peak, India will be the most populous country in the world. China at its peak in 2025 will have 1.395 billion (139.5 crore) people. In fact, when China peaks, India will have already surpassed it in population.

Population of India increased from 103 crore in 2001 to 121 crore in 2011, an increase of 18 crore or 17.6 percent. Out of 121 crore, 62.4 crore were males and 58.6 crore were females.

More precisely, India added 18.1 crore people to its population between 2001 and 2011 against 18.2 crore in the preceding decade. However, even 18.1 crore equals the total population of Brazil, the world's fifth most populous country.

For the first time since Independence in 1947, India added fewer people to its population in the decade just ended (2001-2011) than in the previous one. While decadal population growth rates have consistently been declining since the 1960s, the absolute addition in each decade was always higher than in the previous decade. That is now changed.

At 121 crore, India's population is almost equal to the combined population of US, Indonesia, Brazil, Pakistan,

Bangladesh and Japan. Mainland China's population is 135 crore.

The unabated growth of population is attributable to a sharp decline in death-rate coupled with relatively high birth rate. The death rate (7.1 per thousand in 2011) has fallen due to improved health conditions, control of epidemics, better handling of famine conditions, and general improvement in the standard of living. There has been a significant decline in the infant mortality rate since Independence.

However, birth rate in India is still very high (21.8 per thousand in 2011). Many social and economic factors are responsible for high birth-rate. These include universality of marriage, preference for male children, illiteracy, and poverty. The rapid growth of population has seriously hampered developmental efforts.

The projections of population made by National Commission for Enterprises in the Unorganized Sector (NCEUS) in its report titled *The Challenge of Employment in India: An Informal Economy Perspective* (April 2009) are presented in Table 10.1.

Table 10.1: Projected Population and Growth Rates in Different Years by Sex

(million)

Year	Male	Female	Total
2002	541.68	505.30	1046.98
2007	584.78 (1.54)	545.19 (1.53)	1129.97 (1.54)
2012	626.63 (1.39)	583.70 (1.37)	1210.32 (1.38)
2017	665.48 (1.21)	619.41 (1.19)	1284.89 (1.20)

Source: National Commission for Enterprises in the Unorganized Sector (NCEUS), *The Challenge of Employment in India: An Informal Economy Perspective*, April 2009, Volume I, Table 5.1, p. 104.

10.2 Characteristics of India's Population

These are as under:

10.2.1 Age Composition: Age composition of population is important because it indicates the dependency ratio of the population. Dependency ratio is defined as the ratio of children below 15 years to population above 15 years. The age composition also determines the proportion of the labour force (15-60 years) in the total population. Projections of total population and its age structure are given in Table 10.2. Due to expected decline in fertility and mortality, the age structure of the population will change in the future.

Table 10.2: Projections of Age Structure of India's Population
(million)

Year	2006	2011	2016	2021	2026
Total	1112 (100.0)	1193 (100.0)	1269 (100.0)	1340 (100.0)	1400 (100.0)
Below 15 years	357 (32.1)	347 (29.1)	340 (26.8)	337 (25.1)	327 (23.4)
15-64 years	699 (62.9)	780 (65.4)	851 (67.1)	908 (67.8)	957 (68.3)
Above 65 years	56 (5.0)	66 (5.5)	78 (6.1)	95 (7.1)	116 (8.3)

Figures in parentheses are percentages of respective totals.
Source: Government of India, *Economic Survey*, 2006-07, p. 215, Table 10.7 (excerpted).

10.2.2 Overall Sex Ratio: The census also records overall sex ratio, which is the number of females to every 1,000 males across all ages. In 1921, the number of females per thousand males was 955. There were many reasons for excess of male over female population. The lack of pre-natal and post-natal care was the major cause of high death-rate among women in reproductive age. The evil practice of female infanticide in some parts of the country during British rule also contributed to reduced share of female population in total population.

Even during the post-Independence period, the trend of sex ratio in India has been in favour of masculine population. According to the 1991 census, there were 927 females per thousand males. As per 2001 Census, the sex ratio stood at 933 females per 1,000 males, a marginal improvement over 1991.

The persistent tendency towards low sex ratio can be attributed to lack of attention and care given to female children, sex selective female abortions, and the higher death-rate among women in the reproductive age. It is noteworthy that in Western countries, the sex ratio favours the feminine population.

Improved medical technology, education and improvement in quality of life during the first decade of the 21st century resulted in the overall gender ratio improving from 933 in 2001 to 940 in 2011. This is in line with general improvement in the overall sex ratio since 1991. Only 3 major states showed a decline in their sex ratio: J&K, Bihar and Gujarat.

Delhi and Haryana are the states with the worst overall sex ratios (866 and 877 respectively). In fact, a healthy sex ratio remains largely a southern phenomenon. Kerala is the only state where women outnumber men (1,084 females for every 1,000 males). Next in order is Tamil Nadu with 995 females for every 1.000 males.

10.2.3 Child Sex Ratio (0-6 years): The data show that the sex ratio for children below 6 years (i.e. number of girls for every 1,000 boys) dropped from 927 in 2001 to a dismal 914 in 2011. This decline is unabated since 1961 Census. Among big states, Chhattisgarh has the highest child sex ratio of 964 followed by Kerala with 959. Haryana is at the bottom (830) followed by Punjab (846). This gender bias draws attention to a lingering societal flaw which economic growth is not being able to correct.

As a result of this declining sex ratio, millions of girls/women are missing in India. It is an alarming scenario and if this trend continues, violence against women would increase and there would be forced polyandry. The demographic balance would be permanently damaged.

One of the reasons for the declining sex ratios is the incidence of sex selection, and or sex determination followed by sex selective abortions. This constitutes a grave form of discrimination against women as women are affected as being part of a social class. This is not a pro-life or pro-choice issue. A woman's right to abortion has to be upheld on grounds of promoting women's rights to equality. The right to abortion is the right to abort any foetus. The abortion of a female foetus following a sex determination test is an act of discrimination. As this act of discrimination cannot be committed without the active intervention of medical professionals, it is essential to strictly enforce laws directed towards regulating the practice of medical professionals. However, keeping in mind the pressures that a woman is subjected to for bearing a male child, the implementation and enforcement of such laws should not lead to the further victimization of women.

The laws regulating sex determination and abortions are provided for in the Pre-conception and Pre-natal Diagnostic Techniques (Prohibition of Misuse) Act and the Medical Termination of Pregnancies Act, 1971. In addition, penal provisions on "causing miscarriages" are also provided in Sections 312-316 of the Indian Penal Code.

Sex determination before birth is widely prevalent. Certain districts in Punjab and Haryana account for a substantial drop in the decennial child sex ratio. Richer districts tend to account for a larger decline in the child sex ratio. The incidence of the use of sex determination techniques tends to be more in the most modern and developed districts. This calls into question the argument that the market economy undermines patriarchal authoritarian and male-biased traditional attitudes and spreads egalitarian values. Policy has to address the concern that inculcation of the values of market economy seems to be only enhancing gender inequity as reflected in the female foeticide and infanticide indicators.

There are two important issues of policy associated with this decline in the child sex ratio. One is the obsession with population control, which assumes that all the failures in development can be mono-causally linked to population explosion. The other more recent issue is the intrusion of the two-child norm into the Panchayati Raj Acts of many states, despite its absence from the Population Policy of 2000, leading to disqualification of many elected representatives. Most of the excluded belong to the scheduled castes (SCs) and scheduled tribes (STs). Some experts have suggested a link between the imposition of the two-child norm and sex selective abortions. Imposition of the two-child norm, then, cannot be the route to population stabilisation, for it may lead to a disturbingly unbalanced population.

10.2.4 Life Expectancy: Life expectancy in India at birth stood at 66.1 during 2006-10. The life expectancy has improved after Independence owing to decline in infant mortality, control of epidemics, and general improvement in the standard of living. Life expectancy of both males and females is projected to increase in the coming decades. The most fundamental of all human capabilities is life itself and the steady rise in life expectation in the country suggests that significant progress has been made in this dimension. Life expectancy which was only 32 years at the time of Independence is now 67 years. In other words, every Indian can expect to live twice as long as was the case at Independence! Nevertheless, the level of life expectancy in India remains lower than in many emerging market economies and it is appropriate to plan for significant further improvements in this important dimension.

Increasing longevity will inevitably bring in its wake increase in the prevalence of non-communicable diseases. The growing number of senior citizens in the country poses a major challenge and the cost of providing socio-economic security and healthcare to this population has to be met. Currently several region and culture-specific innovative interventions to provide needed care to this population are underway and among these are efforts to reverse the trend of break up of joint families. If these efforts succeed, it will be possible to provide necessary care for rapidly increasing population of senior citizens within the resources of the family and the country. Majority of the people in their sixties will be physically and psychologically fit and would like to participate both in economic and social activities. They should be encouraged and supported to lead a productive life and contribute to the national development. Senior citizens in their seventies and beyond and those with health problems would require assistance. So far, the families have borne major share in caring for the elderly. This should remain the ideal method. However, there is growing number of elderly without family support. For them, alternate modes for caring may have to be evolved and implemented.

10.2.5 Literacy Rate: Literacy is an important factor in judging the quality of population. Illiteracy is widespread in rural areas as compared to urban areas. Therefore, concerted efforts are needed to direct literacy programmes towards rural areas with particular emphasis on female literacy.

The census definition of literacy is the ability to both read and write in any language. The population below 6 years is not counted as they are considered illiterate irrespective of their ability to read or write.

India's literacy rate for people aged 6 and older increased to 74 percent nationwide in 2011, from 65 percent in 2001. However, this was well short of the target set by the Planning Commission to achieve a literacy rate of over 85 percent by 2011-12.

Kerala has the highest literacy rate at 94 percent while Bihar the lowest at 64 percent.

For males, literacy rate rose to 82.2 percent in 2011 from 75 percent in 2001. For females, it went up to 65.5 percent in 2011 from 54 percent in 2001.

In fact, the gap in literacy between men and women got reduced to an all-time low of just 16.7 percentage points in 2011. In 2001, this gap was 21 percentage points.

Data of Census 2011 affirms the India growth story— population growth slowing down and the number of literates growing, especially female literates. The census definition of literacy is the ability to both read and write in any language. The population below 6 years is not counted as they are considered illiterate irrespective of their ability to read or write.

10.2.6 Degree of Urbanisation: Urbanisation is directly associated with economic development. In fact, a shift of population from rural to urban areas is an indicator of economic development. The shift of population to urban areas was slow during British rule, signifying that the process of economic development itself was slow during that period. Urban population which formed 10 percent of total population in 1911, moderately increased to 14 percent in 1941. This was in sharp contrast to the urbanisation trend taking place in Europe.

India ranks poorly among the countries of the world in respect of degree of urbanisation. The share of urban population in total population was 25.7 percent in 1991 which increased to 27.8 percent in 2001. In 2011, it was 31.2 percent. With prospect of industrialisation and the consequent migration of rural population to urban areas, the trend toward urbanisation will gain momentum.

As the proportion of the urban population continues to grow, investments in urban infrastructure for the provision of services such as roads, water supply and sewerage, urban transportation and the like will need to be much higher than they have been in the past.

Compared to other developing countries, India has been slow to urbanise, but the pace of urbanisation is expected to accelerate over the next two decades. The 2011 Census also shows an increase in the urban population from 27.8 percent in 2001 to 31.2 percent in 2011, and it is likely to exceed 40.0 percent by 2030. This would generate a heavy demand for better quality infrastructure in urban areas, especially water, sewerage, public transport and low cost housing. Since it takes time to create urban infrastructure, it is necessary to have a sufficiently long-term focus on urban planning in the Twelfth Plan.

Like many other demographic changes, urbanization has

both positive and negative effects. Cities and towns have become the engines of social change and rapid economic development. Urbanisation is associated with improved access to education, employment, and healthcare, resulting in increase in the age at marriage, reduction in family size and improvement in health indices. As people have moved towards and into cities, information has flowed outward. Better communication and transportation now link urban and rural areas both economically and socially creating an urban-rural continuum of communities with improvement in some aspects of lifestyle of both.

The ever increasing reach of mass media communicates new ideas, points of reference, and available options are becoming more widely recognized, appreciated and sought. This phenomenon has affected healthcare, including reproductive health, in many ways. For example, radio and television programmes that discuss gender equity, family size preference and family planning options are now reaching formerly isolated rural populations. This can create demand for services for mothers and children, higher contraceptive use, and fewer unwanted pregnancies, smaller healthier families and lead to more rapid population stabilisation.

However, the rapid growth of urban population also poses some serious challenges. Urban population growth has outpaced the development of basic minimum services. Housing, water supply, sewerage and solid waste disposal are far from adequate. Increasing waste generation at home, offices and industries, coupled with poor waste disposal facilities result in rapid environmental deterioration. Increasing automobiles add to air pollution. All these have adverse effect on ecology and health. Poverty persists in urban and peri-urban areas. Awareness about the glaring inequities in close urban setting may lead to social unrest. As a consequence cities are facing the problem of expanding urban slums.

10.2.7 Density of Population: Density of population means the average number of persons living per squire kilometre of area. The density of population has increased steadily from 117 persons in 1951 to 216 persons in 1981, to 274 persons in 1991. It increased from 325 persons in 2001 to 382 in 2011, an increase of 17.5 percent. Since density of population indicates the land-man ratio, it is clear that this ratio has been declining over the years.

10.3 Demographic Dividend Hypothesis

There is a thinking that if the massive population of India is properly educated and trained, it can prove a boon for the national economy. India's demographic dividend is essentially due to two factors: (a) declining birth rates and (b) improvement in life expectancy. The declining birth rate changes the age distribution and makes for a smaller proportion of population in the dependent ages and for relatively larger share in the productive labour force. The result is low dependency ratio which can provide comparative cost advantage and competitiveness to the economy. Moreover, the global economy is expected to witness a skilled manpower shortage to the extent of around 56 million by 2020. Thus, the *demographic dividend* in India needs to be exploited not only to expand the production possibility frontier but also to meet the skilled manpower requirements of India and other countries.

In the longer run, there is another important potential strength arising from our demographic trends. Our dependency rate (ratio of dependent to working age population) is falling whereas that of industrialised countries and even China is rising. The presence of a skilled young population in an environment where investment is expanding and the industrial world ageing could be a major advantage. It is, however, important to realise that we can only reap this demographic dividend if we invest massively on human resource development and skill formation and create an economic environment capable of absorbing our relatively young working population in productive employment.

India has a younger population not only in comparison to advanced economies but also in relation to the large developing countries. As a result, the labour force in India is expected to increase by 32 percent over the next 20 years, while it will decline by 4.0 percent in industrialised countries and by nearly 5.0 percent in China. This demographic dividend can add to growth potential, provided two conditions are fulfilled. First, higher levels of health, education and skill development must be achieved. Second, an environment must be created in which the economy not only grows rapidly, but also enhances good quality employment/livelihood opportunities to meet the needs and aspirations of the youth.

10.4 Areas of Concern and Future Challenges

Although India has the advantage of a large pool of human resources, the industry continues to face deficit in manpower possessing the right skills for manufacturing, service, marketing etc. State level institutions such as district industries centres (DICs), which could play an important role in capacity building, have been unable to transform themselves from regulating bodies to facilitating agencies. Their current infrastructure is sub-optimally utilised.

The development of the small-scale sector has been hampered due to the shortage of trained and experienced managerial and supervisory personnel. Provision of technical services is needed to stimulate productive efficiency and new product lines. Most MSMEs do not have money to invest in market research and are unable to carry out design and technical improvements to keep up with market demands. Unlike big businesses, they cannot invest in advertising and packaging. This limits their ability to tap markets and attract consumers. MSMEs, especially those pertaining to traditional livelihoods are, therefore, increasingly being forced to rely on middle men, petty traders and big businesses to market their products.

Lack of skilled manpower and information as well as lack

of reach to modern technology are key issues affecting the growth of MSME sector. It is often said that India enjoys a *demographic dividend* compared to rest of the world due to its huge population in productive age group. Most of the other developed as well as developing countries face the threat of an aging population. If this comparative advantage can be augmented with adequate skill development, India can become the global supplier of quality manpower. In this backdrop, the Government has decided to accord top priority to skill development.

The country, however, has a big challenge ahead as it is estimated that only 4.69 percent of the total workforce in India has undergone formal skill training as compared to 68 percent in UK, 75 percent in Germany, 52 percent in USA, 80 percent in Japan and 96 percent in South Korea. While the debate on the exact quantum of the challenge continues, there is no disputing the fact that it is indeed a challenge of formidable proportion.

One of the major challenges in the country today is public perception on skilling, which is viewed as the last option meant for those who have not been able to progress in the formal academic system. A number of factors are responsible for this state of affairs:

1. Social and traditional view that sees status as being inversely proportional to the degree to which one works with one's hands. This can also be attributed to primeval and archaic ethos which compartmentalized the skilling landscape for several hundred years. This unfortunate legacy has no moral, ethical and constitutional sanction in free India. Nonetheless, this gets at times manifested in norms, attitudes and societal behaviour.
2. The proclivity of large sections of industry especially in the micro, small and medium sectors to treat skilled and unskilled persons at par, thereby depriving skilling of any meaningful economic incentive.
3. Most of the vocational training programmes are not

aligned to the requirements of the industry As a result of the above, a piquant situation exists in the country wherein unemployment continues to coexist with lack of requisite number of skilled people at functional level to build roads and bridges, lay pipelines, work in factories, engage in offshore drilling, build ships etc.

Different states in India face varied challenges in relation to demographics and skill development. There needs to be a shared sense of urgency to address the challenges of the changing demography. While State Skill Development Missions (SSDMs) have been launched in almost all States, there is an imminent need for capacity building and empowerment of SSDMs in many States in order to upscale quality skill development.

The various grant-based, free training programmes available today, though necessary, have their own limitations especially on quality and employability. Students undergoing training for free attach little value to training whereas training providers focus on increasing their numbers rather than quality of training. While financial support is required for certain industry sectors or segments of unorganised sector, it is critical to exercise utmost discretion and link employability with all such efforts.

There is multiplicity in assessment and certification systems existing in the country which leads to inconsistent outcomes and causes confusion to the employers. The availability of good quality trainers is a major area of concern. There is a lack of focus on development of trainer training programmes and career progression pathways for trainers have also not been defined.

Efforts in the skill landscape have been largely devoid of industry/employer linkages until the last few years. This has created gaps in terms of sectoral need and availability, competency required by employer and those possessed by a trainee etc. Placement of trainees has consequently suffered. While industry has started defining their skills requirements, and training methodology, commitments in terms of increased remuneration to skilled workers also need to be made by them. This is necessary to create economic incentive for skilling, and for industry to realize the productivity gains linked with skilled manpower.

One of the biggest challenges of skill development in our country is that 93 percent of the workforce is in the unorganized/informal sector. Consequently it is difficult to map existing skills in the unorganised sector and gauge the skilling requirement in the sector. On the other hand, the rate of job growth in informal sector is estimated to be twice that in formal sector.

Women constitute almost half of the demographic dividend. The key challenge here is to increase their participation in the country's labour force, which is directly linked to economic growth of the country. Mainstreaming gender roles by skilling women in non-traditional roles and increasing gender sensitivity in the workplace will have a catalytic effect on productivity.

Job creation for skilled youth is also a major challenge before the nation. Entrepreneurship based on innovation has immense growth potential. However, the number of local entrepreneurs emerging every year in India is very low. Accelerating entrepreneurship especially that based on innovation is crucial for large-scale employment generation in India.

11

Institutional Set-up for HRD in India

As India moves progressively towards becoming a global knowledge economy, it must meet the rising aspirations of its youth. This can be partially achieved through focus on advancement of skills that are relevant to the emerging economic environment. The challenge pertains not only to a huge quantitative expansion of the facilities for skill training, but also to the equally important task of raising their quality.

Skills and knowledge are driving forces of economic growth and social development for any country. Countries with higher levels and better standards of skills adjust more effectively to the challenges and opportunities in domestic and international job markets. For a skills strategy to be successful, it should be complemented by commensurate creation of jobs in the primary, secondary and tertiary sectors.

Skill development, however, cannot be viewed in isolation. Skills are germane to, but not always sufficient for securing adequate economic dividends. Skills need to be an integral part of employment and economic growth strategies to spur employability and productivity. Coordination with other national macroeconomic paradigms and growth strategies is therefore critical.

Skill development programmes of the Central Government over the years have been spread across more than 20 Ministries/Departments without any robust coordination and monitoring mechanism to ensure convergence. The scenario is no different in most of the states except the few states which have moved towards functional convergence by creating State Missions. This legacy has resulted in multiplicity of norms, procedures, curricula, certifications etc. Further, many of these skill development initiatives often remain unaligned to demand, thus defeating its entire objective.

Three important Ministries of the Central Government which deal with skill development schemes and programmes are the following.
1. Ministry of Human Resource Development (MHRD).
2. Ministry of Labour and Employment.
3. Ministry of Skill Development and Entrepreneurship (MSDE).

11.1 Ministry of Human Resource Development (MHRD)

MHRD was created on September 26, 1985. Currently, the MHRD works through two departments:
- Department of School Education and Literacy.
- Department of Higher Education.

Department of School Education and Literacy is responsible for development of school education and literacy in the country. It has its eyes set on the *universalisation of education* and making better citizens out of India's young brigade. For this, various new schemes and initiatives are taken up regularly and recently, those schemes and initiatives have also started paying dividends in the form of growing enrolment in schools.

Department of Higher Education takes care of what is one of the largest higher education systems of the world, just after the United States and China. It is engaged in bringing world class opportunities of higher education and research to the country so that Indian students are not found lacking when facing an international platform. For this, the Government has launched joint ventures and signed MoUs to help the Indian students benefit from the world opinion.

The main objectives of MHRD are as under:
1. Formulating the national policy on education and to ensure that it is implemented in letter and spirit.
2. Planned development, including expanding access and improving quality of the educational institutions throughout the country, including the regions where

people do not have easy access to education.
3. Paying special attention to disadvantaged groups like the poor, females and the minorities.
4. Provide financial help in the form of scholarships, loan subsidy etc. to deserving students from deprived sections of the society.
5. Encouraging international co-operation in the field of education, including working closely with the UNESCO and foreign governments as well as universities, to enhance the educational opportunities in the country.

11.2 Ministry of Labour and Employment

Ministry of Labour and Employment is one of the oldest and important Ministries of the Government of India. The main responsibility of the Ministry is to protect and safeguard the interests of workers in general and the poor, deprived and disadvantaged sections of the society, in particular. Further it aims to creating a healthy work environment for higher production and productivity and to develop and coordinate vocational skill training and employment.

The vision of the Ministry is: (a) to provide decent working conditions and improved quality of life of workers, (b) ensuring India without child labour in hazardous sectors and (c) enhancing employability through employment services and skill development on a sustainable basis.

Its mission is: (a) improving the working conditions and the quality of life of workers through laying down and implementing policies, programmes, schemes and projects for providing social security and welfare measures, (b) regulating conditions of work, occupational health and safety of workers, (c) eliminating child labour from hazardous occupations and processes, (d) strengthening enforcement of labour laws and (e) promoting skill development and employment services.

At present, there are 44 labour related statutes enacted by the Central Government dealing with minimum wages, accidental and social security benefits, occupational safety and health, conditions of employment, disciplinary action, formation of trade unions, industrial relations, etc. Government's attention is also focused on promotion of welfare and providing social security to the labour force both in organized and unorganized sectors, in tandem with the process of liberalization. These objectives are sought to be achieved through implementation of various labour laws, which regulate the terms and conditions of service and employment of workers. The State Governments are also empowered to enact legislations, as labour is a subject in the concurrent list under the Constitution of India.

11.3 Ministry of Skill Development and Entrepreneurship (MSDE)

India presently faces a dual challenge of paucity of highly trained workforce, as well as non-employability of large sections of the conventionally educated youth, who possess little or no job skills. Ministry for Skill Development and Entrepreneurship (earlier Department of Skill Development and Entrepreneurship notified in July 2014) was set up in November 2014 to give fresh impetus to the Skill India agenda and help create an appropriate ecosystem that facilitates imparting employable skills to its growing workforce over the next few decades. Apart from meeting its own demand, India has the potential to provide skilled workforce to fill the expected shortfall in the ageing developed world.

The Ministry is responsible for co-ordination of all skill development efforts across the country, removal of disconnect between demand and supply of skilled manpower, building the vocational and technical training framework, skill up-gradation, building of new skills, and innovative thinking not only for existing jobs but also jobs that are to be created. The Ministry aims to achieve its vision of a 'Skilled India'. It is aided in these initiatives by its following functional arms:
1. National Skill Development Corporation (NSDC).
2. National Skill Development Fund (NSDF).
3. National Skill Development Agency (NSDA).

There are 33 sector skill councils (SSCs) as well as 187 training partners registered with NSDC. The Ministry also works with the existing network of skill development centres, universities and other alliances in the field. Further, it collaborates with relevant Central Ministries, State Governments, international organizations, industry and NGOs for multi-level engagement and more impactful implementation of skill development efforts.

The Ministry has been allocated the following business:

1. Co-ordination with all concerned for evolving an appropriate skill development framework, removal of disconnect between the demand for and supply of skilled manpower through vocational and technical training, skill up-gradation, building of new skills, innovative thinking and talents not only for the existing jobs but also the jobs that are to be created.
2. Mapping of existing skills and their certification.
3. Expansion of youth entrepreneurship education and capacity through forging strong partnership between educational institutions, business and other community organizations and set national standards for it.
4. Role of co-ordination relating to skill development.
5. Doing market research and devising training curriculum in important sectors.
6. Industry-Institute linkages.
7. Bringing public-private-partnership (PPP) element in this activity—partnership with the industries which need the skilled manpower.
8. Making broad policies for all other Ministries/Departments with regard to market requirements and skill development.
9. Framing policies for soft skills.
10. Skill development related to information technology (IT) and computer education.
11. Academic equivalence of skill sets.
12. Skilling for entrepreneurship development for science and technology.

13. Work relating to Industrial Training Institutes (ITIs).
14. National Skill Development Corporation.
15. National Skill Development Agency.
16. National Skill Development Fund.
17. National Institute for Entrepreneurship and Small Business Development, NOIDA.
18. Indian Institute of Entrepreneurship, Guwahati.

11.3.1 National Skill Development Corporation (NSDC): The first National Policy on Skill Development was notified in 2009. In the aftermath of this policy, National Skill Development Corporation (NSDC) was established in 2009 to promote private sector participation via innovative funding models. NSDC has tied up with more than 211 training providers, many of whom have started scaling up their operations, to offer short-term training programmes. They also supported and incubated 37 sector skills councils (SSCs) which are intended to facilitate much needed participation and ownership of industry to ensure needs based training programmes.

NSDC is a public-private-partnership (PPP) initiative in India. It aims to promote skill development by catalyzing creation of large, quality, for-profit vocational institutions. NSDC provides funding to build scalable, for-profit vocational training initiatives. Its mandate is to enable support systems such as quality assurance, information systems and train the trainer academies either directly or through partnerships. NSDC acts as a catalyst in skill development by providing funding to enterprises, companies and organisations that provide skill training. It also develops appropriate models to enhance, support and coordinate private sector initiatives. The differentiated focus for the 21 sectors under NSDC's purview and its understanding of their viability makes every sector attractive to private investment.

NSDC is a not-for-profit company set up by the Ministry of Finance, under Section 25 of the Companies Act. It has an equity base of ₹ 10 crore, of which the Government of India holds 49 percent, while the private sector has the balance 51 percent.

NSDC has two-tier structure, viz. a 15 member board and

a National Skill Development Fund (NSDF) as a 100 percent Government-owned trust to facilitate its mandate of coordinating and stimulating private sector initiative in the area of skill development with enhanced flexibility and effectiveness.

A. Vision: NSDC was set up as part of a national skill development mission to fulfil the growing need in India for skilled manpower across sectors and narrow the existing gap between the demand and supply of skills. The Union Finance Minister announced the formation of the National Skill Development Corporation (NSDC) in his Budget Speech (2008-09): "There is a compelling need to launch a world-class skill development programme in a mission mode that will address the challenge of imparting the skills required by a growing economy. Both the structure and the leadership of the mission must be such that the programme can be scaled up quickly to cover the whole country".

B. Mission:
1. Upgrade skills to international standards through significant industry involvement and develop necessary frameworks for standards, curriculum and quality assurance.
2. Enhance, support and co-ordinate private sector initiatives for skill development through appropriate public-private-partnership (PPP) models; and strive for significant operational and financial involvement from the private sector.
3. Play the role of a *market-maker* by bringing financing, particularly in sectors where market mechanisms are ineffective or missing.
4. Prioritize initiatives that can have a multiplier or catalytic effect as opposed to one-off impact.

C. Objective: NSDC was formed to achieve the target of skilling/up-skilling 150 million people by 2022 by fostering private sector initiatives in the skill development space. NSDC along with the support of its 31 sector skill councils and 136 training partners works continuously in collaboration with each other, to create a successful model for the country which is being evaluated periodically for improvement and effectiveness.

To ensure superior decision-making, the NSDC requires a structure and governance model that provides it with autonomy, stature and continuity. Thus, the organisation has a tiered decision-making structure:

D. Functions: NSDC plays three key roles:

- **Funding and Incentivising**: In the near term this is a key role. This involves providing financing either as loans or equity, providing grants and supporting financial incentives to select private sector initiatives to improve financial viability through tax breaks etc. The exact nature of funding (equity, loan and grant) depends on the viability or attractiveness of the segment and, to some extent, the type of player (for-profit private, non-profit industry association or non-profit NGO). Over time, the NSDC aspires to create strong viable business models and reduce its grant-making role.
- **Enabling Support Services**: A skills development institute requires a number of inputs or support services such as curriculum, faculty and their training, standards and quality assurance, technology platforms, student placement mechanisms and so on. The NSDC plays a significant enabling role in some of these support services, most importantly and in the near-term, setting up standards and accreditation systems in partnership with industry associations.
- **Shaping/Creating**: In the near-term, the NSDC proactively provides momentum for large-scale participation by private players in skill development. NSDC identifies critical skill groups, develops models for skill development and attracts potential private players and provides support to these efforts.

E. Advocacy and Communications: NSDC has a robust communications strategy to keep the momentum of the programme going and also encourage young people to come forward and get skilled. There is constant creation of content and marketing material (poster campaign, STAR animation video, TVC's etc.) which is available with NSDC which the partners and all other stakeholders can use to talk about their skilling programme.

NSDC launched its advertisement campaign *Hunar Hai to Kadar Hai* with two television commercials which aired in February-March 2014. These TVCs talked about the success stories of real people with real ambitions in the automotive and retail sector, and are available for marketing purpose.

A helpline number 088000-55555 which was announced during the TVC, link potential trainees with the nearby training centres and educate them about the offerings of the programme. NSDC is also actively engaging with all its stakeholder holders on social media platform.

F. Innovation and Engagement Units: The innovation and engagement practice within NSDC has two key focus areas. The innovation unit is focused on supporting high impact and innovative solutions that can disrupt the skilling ecosystem and/or enhance outcomes manifold, preferably in sectors and regions with unmet needs. The engagement unit works with both internal and external stakeholders to strengthen the skills ecosystem, thus contributing to the larger NSDC mission.

(a) Innovation Unit: In the effort to meet the incremental demands in vocational skills, evaluate past efforts and generate new ideas, this unit looks at sustainable ideas that can add value to the vocational training ecosystem across various categories under the larger skills framework. Based on the understanding of the ecosystem, the following 4 key areas have been identified for support:
1. Sourcing and financing.
2. Training to certification.
3. Placement and linkages.
4. Post-placement support.

(b) Engagement Unit: The activities of the engagement

unit can broadly be classified as below:
- **Assistance:** The team works with partners that are under-performing to assist them in strengthening their business plans through deep dive analysis and external support through a select group of turnaround specialists. It also carries out business restructuring in cases where there is continuous under-performance and the initial plan targets might not be met during the term period.
- **External Engagement:** The team works with multiple stakeholders including corporates, foundations, corporate social responsibility (CSR) arms, impact funds, incubators, market facilitators etc. to design and support high impact collaborative projects to enhance skilling outcomes, thus achieving multiplier effect.

G. Corporate Social Responsibility (CSR) for Skill Development: NSDC works with corporates, foundations, government, and community-based organizations in structuring high impact collaborative projects.

The Companies Act, 2013, which came into effect on April 1, 2014, lists corporate social responsibility (CSR) mandate for Indian companies.

The 2013 Act makes an effort to introduce the culture of corporate social responsibility (CSR) in Indian corporates by requiring companies to formulate a corporate social responsibility policy and at least incur a given minimum expenditure on social activities.

It may be recalled that the Ministry of Corporate Affairs (MCA) had introduced the Corporate Social Responsibility Voluntary Guidelines in 2009. These guidelines have now been incorporated within the 2013 Act and have obtained legal sanctity. Section 135 of the 2013 Act, seeks to provide that every company having a net worth of ₹ 500 crore, or more or a turnover of ₹ 1,000 crore or more, or a net profit of ₹ 5 crore or more, during any financial year shall constitute the corporate social responsibility committee of the board. This committee needs to comprise of three or more directors, out of which, at

least one director should be an independent director. The composition of the committee shall be included in the board's report. The committee shall formulate the policy, including activities specified in Schedule VII, which are as follows:
1. Eradicating extreme hunger and poverty.
2. Promotion of education.
3. Promoting gender equality and empowering women.
4. Reducing child mortality and improving maternal health.
5. Combating human immunodeficiency virus, acquired immune deficiency syndrome, malaria and other diseases.
6. Ensuring environmental sustainability.
7. Employment enhancing vocational skills.
8. Social business projects.
9. Contribution to the Prime Minister's National Relief Fund or any other fund set-up by the central government or the state governments for socio-economic development and relief, and funds for the welfare of the scheduled castes and tribes, other backward classes, minorities and women.
10. Such other matters as may be prescribed.

There have been mixed reactions to the introduction of the 'spend or explain' approach taken by the MCA with respect to CSR. It may take a while before all of corporate India imbibes CSR as a culture.

However, activities specified in the Schedule are not elaborate or detailed enough to indicate the kind of projects that could be undertaken, for example, environment sustainability or social business projects could encompass a wide range of activities.

The committee will also need to recommend the amount of expenditure to be incurred and monitor the policy from time-to-time. The board shall disclose the contents of the policy in its report, and place it on the website, if any, of the company. The 2013 Act mandates that these companies would be required to spend at least 2 percent of the average net profits of the immediately preceding three years on CSR activities, and if not spent, explanation for the reasons thereof would need to be given in the director's report (Section 135 of the 2013 Act).

NSDC has evolved a robust framework to solicit funds for skill development projects in line with these guidelines. NSDC can assist any entity to design structure and manage skill development projects due to its nation-wide presence through its training organizations. The project can be structured through a direct bipartite agreement, or a tripartite agreement with contributions to the National Skill Development Fund, a Government of India fund under the Ministry of Skill Development and Entrepreneurship. All projects are implemented through approved training partners of NSDC, with monitoring and reporting of project outcomes provided centrally by NSDC. NSDC actively participates in CSR discussions to advocate for skill development through outreach events, industry forums, one-on-one consultations and other ways.

11.3.2 National Skill Development Fund (NSDF): Skill development brings return to the individual, the employing enterprise and the economy as a whole. Therefore, all stakeholders—Government, both at Centre and States, public and private enterprises, and the direct beneficiary, i.e. the individual—should share the burden of mobilizing financial or in-kind resources for skill development.

NSDF, operating arm of the NSDC, was created in 2009 with a corpus of ₹ 995.10 crore as Government-owned trust to receive financial contributions from donors, private entities, governments (both Central and State), statutory bodies, financial institutions etc. NSDC and NSDF would enter into an investment management agreement whereby NSDF would provide funds to NSDC for furtherance of the objective of skill development in accordance with the approved work and financial plan. NSDC would charge a management fee from NSDF for managing its resources. The beneficiaries of the trust are the youth of India who require skill development and vocational training. Its main functions are as follows:
1. Making periodic as well as an annual report of its plans and activities and put them in the public domain.

2. Establishing a trainee placement and tracking system for effective evaluation and future policy planning.
3. Establishing credible independent certification systems for both vocational education (VE) and vocational training (VT) with the scope for permitting vertical and horizontal mobility within and between VE and VT.

The Fund is contributed by various Government sources, and other donors/contributors to enhance, stimulate and develop the skills of Indian youth by various sector-specific programmes. A public trust, set up by the Government of India, is the custodian of the Fund. The Trust accepts donations, contributions in cash or kind from the contributors for furtherance of objectives of the Fund. The Fund is operated and managed by the board of trustees. The chief executive officer of the trust is responsible for day-to-day administration and management of the Trust.

Accounts of the trust are subject to CAG Audit and are also audited by a Chartered Accountant for every financial year and in such manner as may be directed by Government of India. The Trust has engaged IL&FS Trust Company Ltd (ITCL), one of the largest Corporate Trustees in India, for providing micro prudential oversight on the implementing partner and monitoring the interests of Trust.

The Fund meets its objectives through National Skill Development Corporation (NSDC) which is an industry-led not-for-profit-company set up for building skill development capacity and forging strong linkages with the market. NSDC acts as a catalyst in skill development by providing funding to enterprises, companies and organizations that provide skill training. It also develops appropriate models to enhance, support and coordinate private sector initiatives. Till March 31, 2015, NSDF had released ₹ 2,333 crore to NSDC towards skill development programmes including National Skill Certification and Monetary Reward Scheme (STAR) and UDAAN Scheme (J&K-oriented). NSDC with 160 training partners and 1,722 training centres has so far trained around 35 lakh persons across India.

11.3.3 National Skill Development Agency (NSDA):

NSDA was notified through a gazette notification dated June 6, 2013. NSDA is an autonomous body (registered as a society under the Societies Registration Act, 1860) of Ministry of Skill Development and Entrepreneurship, which coordinates and harmonizes the skill development efforts of the Government and the private sector to achieve the skilling targets. It endeavours to bridge the social, regional, gender and economic divide through the following:

- By ensuring that the skilling needs of the disadvantaged and marginalized groups like SCs, STs, OBCs, minorities, women and differently-abled persons are taken care of through the various skill development programmes.
- By taking affirmative actions as part of advocacy by the NSDA. NSDA anchors the national skills qualifications framework (NSQF) and facilitates the setting up of professional certifying bodies in addition to the existing ones.

A. Functions: NSDA discharges the following functions:

1. Take all possible steps to meet skilling targets as envisaged in the Twelfth Five Year Plan (2012-17) and beyond.
2. Co-ordinate and harmonize the approach to skill development among various Central Ministries/Departments, State Governments, NSDC and the private sector.
3. Anchor and operationalize the NSQF to ensure that quality and standards meet sector-specific requirements.
4. Be the nodal agency for state skill development missions.
5. Raise extra-budgetary resources for skill development from various sources such as international agencies, including multilateral agencies, and the private sector.
6. Evaluate existing skill development schemes with a view to assessing their efficacy and suggest corrective action to make them more effective.
7. Create and maintain a national data base related to skill development including development of a dynamic labour market information system (LMIS).

8. Take affirmative action for advocacy.
9. Ensure that the skilling needs of the disadvantaged and the marginalized groups like SCs, STs, OBCs, minorities, women and differently-abled persons are taken care of.
10. Discharge any other function as may be assigned to it by the Government of India.

B. Other Activities:

(a) **Rationalization of the Skill Development Schemes of the Government of India:** NSDA has worked with the concerned ministries and stakeholders to achieve convergence of norms across the various central schemes for skill development, while at the same time recognizing the special needs of the North-Eastern States, the hill States, and other geographies that pose challenging situations for skill development.

(b) **Creation of an Integrated Labour Market Information System:** A national database on all major aspects of skill development has been created in partnership with all other Ministries of the Government of India and the State Governments. This is a one-shop stop where all the relevant information is freely available to citizens. The government has created a National Steering Committee for setting up the labour market information system (LMIS). The LMIS would bring in operational efficiencies, would be transparent and available to all, and would help reduce considerably the situation of one individual being benefited under different schemes.

(c) **Engagement with States:** NSDA is actively engaged with various State Governments to plan out their skill development action plans, help them develop their skill development policies, and set up suitable administrative mechanisms. Through Technical Assistance Programmes with the Asian Development bank (ADB), European Union (EU) and Department for International Development (DFID) of the Government of UK, NSDA is helping the State Skill Development Missions of various states to build their respective capacities.

(d) Skills Innovation Initiative: A committee has been set up under the Skills Innovation Initiative housed under the NSDA. NSDA invites innovative ideas, concepts and practices on skill development. The Committee reviews all the proposals of innovations to facilitate their application on a wider scale. Selected innovative practices are facilitated and propagated for wider application.

12

Target Groups for Skill Development

Human development insists that everyone should enjoy a minimum level of security. In fact, a system should be built in which the State bears the responsibility for providing and ensuring an elementary or basic level of security, and leaves room for partly or wholly contributory schemes. This will mean that the responsibility to provide a floor will be primarily that of the State, and it will be left to individual citizens to acquire higher levels of security through assumption of responsibility and contributory participation.

The root cause of social insecurity in India is poverty and that is largely due to lack of adequate or productive employment opportunities. The pattern of economic development in India since Independence in 1947 has left in its trail a variety of inequalities which have caused socio-politico tensions. While the economy has performed well in terms of growth rate of gross domestic product (GDP), its performance in terms of human development indicators has been unsatisfactory.

12.1 Skill Development for Marginalized and Vulnerable Groups

Development and empowerment of scheduled castes (SCs), scheduled tribes (STs), other backward classes (OBCs), minorities, disabled and other social groups in order to bring them at par with the rest of society is a commitment enshrined in the Constitution. Policies of the Central and State Governments have tried to ensure equal rights, and access to benefits and resources to disadvantaged groups in society to enable them to develop their potential and capacities as agents of social change, through the process of planned development.

India's recent economic growth performance has, indeed,

been creditable. However, such growth must make a demonstrable difference to the lives of the poorest and most vulnerable citizens. India has the potential and the means to secure a reasonable standard of living for all of its citizens. The socio-economically disadvantaged—particularly women in rural areas—are yet to benefit from development efforts.

Equal access to skill development is essential for all social groups particularly women and disadvantaged section of society, to help them in securing decent employment and moving out of poverty. Removing barriers to access and addressing their specific needs are key elements in achieving inclusive growth. Entry barriers such as educational qualification, transportation, loss of wages, language etc. should be addressed.

While enhancing the opportunity of skill development for all, entry assessments should be deployed to channelize people with different profiles and needs into appropriate skill development programmes. Effort should be combined with a major initiative in raising awareness among the target groups about the benefit of skill development, employment and learning opportunities and also about support schemes that enable them to participate in training. In addition to vocational skills, the provision of soft (or life) skills—including basic literacy, numeracy, occupational safety and health, hygiene, basic labour rights, team work and confidence building—should be made as an integral component of the curricula. This will also help in empowerment of vulnerable groups.

Skill development for employability is an important strategy in the fight against poverty. Accordingly, the poor should have a priority claim and easy access to opportunities for skill development. Efforts in this regard should aim at mitigating the impact of these economic barriers at different stages, as well as actively promote access of the poor to educational and skill development opportunities through specially designed schemes and measures. Such measures—special coaching for competing in admission tests, provision of non-formal skill development opportunities and the expanded provision of scholarships, books and soft-loans—should be developed and implemented. Efforts should be made to better integrate skill development into broader poverty reduction programmes and to strengthen the existing skill development components of such programmes.

12.1.1 Scheduled Castes (SCs): According to 2011 Census, the scheduled castes constituted 16.6 percent of the Indian population. In the past, they have been socially ostracized, economically exploited and denied human dignity and a sense of self-worth. The socio-economic development and protection of SCs from discrimination and exploitation has been a high priority area from the very start of Independent India.

People belonging to SC communities are spread all over the country; almost 80 percent of them live in rural areas. They constitute more than one-fifth of the population of Uttar Pradesh, Punjab, Himachal Pradesh and West Bengal. The State of Punjab has the highest proportion of SCs to the State population. More than half the scheduled caste population is concentrated in the five States of Uttar Pradesh (35.1 million), West Bengal (18.4 million), Tamil Nadu (11.8 million), Andhra Pradesh (12.3 million) and Bihar (13.0 million).

12.1.2 Scheduled Tribes (STs): The population of scheduled tribes (STs) in India stood at 10.42 crore as per the 2011 Census. ST's constitute 8.6 percent of the total population of the country with 91.7 percent of them living in rural areas and 8.3 percent in urban areas. The sex-ratio of ST population in 2001 was 978 which was much higher than the national average of 933. The proportion of the ST population to the total population had also increased from 6.9 percent in 1971 to 8.2 percent in 2001.

The proportion of STs to the total population in States/Union Territories was the highest in the North-Eastern region of Mizoram (94.5 percent) and Lakshadweep (94.5 percent) followed by Nagaland (89.1 percent), Meghalaya

(85.9 percent). Within major states, Chhattisgarh (31.8 percent) had the highest percentage followed by Jharkhand (26.3 percent) and Odisha (22.1 percent). Of the total ST population in the country, Madhya Pradesh accounted for the highest proportion of ST population (14.5 percent) followed by Maharashtra (10.2 percent), Odisha (9.7 percent), Gujarat (8.9 percent), Rajasthan (8.4 percent), Jharkhand (8.4 percent) and Chhattisgarh (7.8 percent). In fact, 68 percent of the country's Scheduled Tribes population lives in these seven States only.

12.1.3 Other Backward Classes (OBCs): Considerable confusion exists regarding the percentage of OBCs population in India's total population. The Second Backward Classes Commission headed by Shri B.P. Mandal (1980), basing its calculation on Census 1931, estimated that other backward classes (OBCs) constituted 52 percent of the population. Recently, NSSO 61st Round (July 2004 to June 2005) report on 'Employment and Unemployment Situation among Social Groups in India' gave an estimate of OBC to constitute 41 percent of the population.

Following measures are needed to help SCs, STs and OBCs to acquire skills and training.

1. Reservations applicable to these groups should be strictly enforced, with appropriate gender composition.
2. Existing schemes for benefiting these groups should be reviewed, strengthened and made more effective.
3. Efforts should be made to mobilize capabilities and expertise of civil society organizations.
4. New innovative schemes and measures should also be devised to ensure full and effective participation by these groups, as well as the accrual of real benefits from skill development initiatives.

12.1.4 Minorities: The Constitution of India contains special provisions for the socio-economic development of the SCs, STs and OBCs [Articles 15(4), 16(4) of Part III, Articles 46 of Part IV, and Articles 330-342 of Part XVI of the Indian Constitution]. However, religious and linguistic minorities are excluded from the purview of these special provisions, though cultural and educational rights of the religious and linguistic minorities are regarded as fundamental rights under Articles 29 and 30 of Part III of the Constitution.

While the socio-economic development of the scheduled castes (SCs), scheduled tribes (STs) and other backward classes (OBCs) formed an important part of the post-Independence development policy, it was presumed that development of the religious and linguistic minorities would be taken care of by the general process of growth and development.

However, the socio-economic conditions of some minorities, particularly Muslims, are a cause for concern.

Following measures are needed to help minorities acquire skills and training.

1. Skill development opportunities for minority groups should be expanded, particularly in minority concentrated areas (MCAs).
2. Existing schemes benefiting these groups should be reviewed, strengthened and made more effective.
3. Efforts should be made to mobilize capabilities and expertise of civil society organizations.
4. Formalization of non-formal skill acquisition and transfer should also be promoted in traditional art and craft sectors.

12.1.5 Persons with Disabilities: The Census 2001, enumerated persons with disabilities, at 2.13 percent of India's total population. According to Eleventh Five Year Plan (2007-12), "The percentage of disabled people among the total population of any country depends on the definition of *disability* in that particular country as well as the enumeration methodology and its accuracy. In India, the definition of disability used in the Census is very different from that in the Persons with Disabilities Act, 1995. There is an urgent need for both a credible definition and system of data collection relating to persons with disabilities. It can be reasonably assumed that persons with disabilities constitute anywhere between 5 to 6 percent of our total population".

Following measures are needed to help them acquire skills and training.
1. The current level of participation of persons with disabilities in skill programmes is very low, despite guidelines of reserving 3 percent of the seats for them. The guidelines apply only to the government sector.
2. People with varying degrees of physical and mental disabilities should be provided with appropriate adjustment training and skills training to bring them in the economic mainstream and make them productive citizens.
3. Training should be integrated with efforts to secure appropriate employment opportunities. Programmes of public awareness and community participation need to be strengthened to promote demand for vocational training by people with disabilities as well as to facilitate their inclusion in the labour market.

12.1.6 School Drop-outs and Child Labour: School drop-outs refer to those who leave the schools before completing XII standard. Following measures are needed to help them acquire skills and training.
1. School education should be strengthened to reduce the school drop outs. The quality of school education should influence the effectiveness of skill development programme as a whole. This will lay solid foundation for young people to acquire employable skills and engage in continuous skill upgradation throughout their working life.
2. School education should be used as a tool to increase vocational awareness among the young people.
3. School drop-outs, child labour and out-of-school youth need to be given alternative education coupled with skill development opportunities to bring them into the economic and social mainstream.
4. Short-term, market-oriented, demand-driven programmes should provide a flexible delivery framework suited to the characteristics and circumstances of the target group.

5. Multi-skilling, multi-entry and exit, and linkages to skill upgradation opportunities in the future, should characterize such programmes. Short-term employable skills need to be expanded greatly to cater to the large size of the group.
6. Formal educational requirements in accessing training should be reviewed in order to facilitate easy access.

12.2 Skill Development for Women Workers

Skill development for employability should be used as an agent of change in promoting women's employment. Women face a multitude of barriers in accessing skills and productive employment, remaining on the job due to effect of globalization or otherwise and advancing to higher level jobs, as well as returning to the labour market after a period of absence, for example, in raising children. A policy of non-discrimination needs to be pursued vigorously to provide equal access for women for skill development and employment.

The problems of women workers in general and in the unorganised sector in particular deserve special emphasis and focus in view of their marginalised position within the class of workers. Even when women are not employed in the sense of contributing to the national output, a considerable share of their time is consumed by socially productive and reproductive labour. This is what is called the *double burden of work* that distinguishes women from men. For women workers in the informal economy, the double burden of combining the tasks of production and reproduction is even more arduous because they are already engaged in activities that require long hours to obtain a subsistence wage.

Thus, while women workers constitute a marginalised category within the class of workers in general, there are layers of subordination determined by structural factors such as the initial conditions of social status and economic sector to which they belong. This is quite evident in the case of women workers in the unorganised sector. There is greater disadvantage for women workers in general and those belonging to rural as well as scheduled castes (SCs)/scheduled tribes (STs) in particular. Apart from such inherited disadvantages as lower social position, a number of other factors also contribute to such a picture. These are their limited asset position, access to resources, and low level of education and skill. Education, and consequently some ability to acquire formal skills, could be a moderating force but this aspect presents a dismal picture. The overall situation of women workers calls for interventions of a promotional nature from different entry points but with a strong emphasis on education.

12.2.1 Education and Women Empowerment: There is an increased awareness that education is one of the most valuable means of achieving gender equality and the empowerment of women. Education is seen as a critical factor in breaking the inter-generational cycle of transmission of poverty. The power of education lies not just in imparting formal literacy, but rather in the acquisition of skills that enable access to multiple literacy—economic, legal, health, political and media etc.

Education is a key intervention in initiating and sustaining processes of empowerment. Good quality education can help women and marginalized communities to: (a) improve their status, (b) enable them to have greater access to information and resources and (c) challenge various forms of discrimination. Education helps strengthen democratic processes as it allows for greater and more equitable participation. Being educated leads to greater self-confidence and self-esteem. It enables engagement with development processes and institutions of governance from a position of strength. Poor women from socially disadvantaged communities are invariably not literate and therefore find themselves at a disadvantage when participating in development processes.

It is, however, important to recognise that while being literate or educated is necessary for empowerment, it does not automatically ensure it. For that a society needs an education system which is of good quality and promotes critical thinking. From the perspective of gender this means that education and literacy should enable women and girls to critically analyse their situations, raise questions about their subordination and help them make informed choices. It is well-known that the institution of schooling is an important site for socialisation that actually reinforces rather than challenges patriarchy and gender discrimination. It is in this context that the content and pedagogy of education become critical considerations.

The focus of educational planning is generally on formal education but this is only one dimension of the educational provisioning, especially when needs of deprived women are under consideration and empowerment of women is the main objective. Though the content of education and classroom pedagogy are critical to altering gender and other social relations it has not been paid the attention it deserves. Efforts to make curricula gender-sensitive have been undertaken but can be considered initial attempts as they have remained largely at the level of removing stereotypes or increasing visibility and have not looked at gender in terms of social relations.

Problems related to the representation of marginalized communities continue to exist and contribute to the deep sense of alienation of these communities from the mainstream education system and a reason for children dropping out. Sexuality is addressed in a problematic manner in educational materials. It is either related to population or reproductive health or seen as a problem associated with promiscuity and shame. Classrooms need to be transformed into spaces that can help girls think critically. Discriminatory practices based on identity-based prejudices need to be monitored and stopped. Corporal punishment, which is wide spread, needs to be checked. The role of the teacher is naturally crucial in this context.

Women, though they make half the world's population, constitute the largest group which is excluded from the benefits of development. Work participation rate of women is much less than that of men. The multiple roles of women and the meagre ability to access resources and available assets are areas of concern. It is important to emphasise that women require adequate security and protection to be self-reliant.

Special attention has to be paid to women workers because of problems peculiar to them. Comparatively speaking, they are much less organised. They also suffer from certain social prejudices and physical disabilities.

12.2.2 Adverse Effects of Globalization on Women: With the growing globalization and liberalization of the economy as well as increased privatization of services, women as a whole have been left behind and not been able to partake of the fruits of success. Mainstreaming of women into the new and emerging areas of growth is imperative. This will require training and skill upgradation in emerging trades, encouraging more women to take up vocational training and employment in the boom sectors. This will also require women to migrate to cities and metros for work. Provision of safe housing and other gender friendly facilities at work will need to be provided.

Another facet of globalization is related to the fact that many persons especially women will be severely affected with the advent of setting up of industrial parks, national highways, special economic zones (SEZs) etc. as huge tracts of farm land are likely to be acquired for this purpose. This would require massive resettlement of the displaced persons and their families. It is therefore essential that a viable resettlement policy and strategy is formulated and put in place immediately which clearly reflects the needs of women impacted by globalization/displacement.

With the removal of all quantitative restrictions on the import of various products, the self-employed women's groups, especially in the informal sector, have started facing competition from the low-priced imported consumer goods which are invading the Indian market. Although this has the imminent danger of displacing a large number of employed and self-employed women, but at the same time, the process of globalization has also opened up opportunities for women entrepreneurs for exporting their products to the markets all over the world. Globalization has thus opened up new challenges for the realization of the goal of women's empowerment. Hence, strategies should be designed to enhance the capacity of women and empower them to cope with the negative economic and social impacts of the globalization process.

Several studies have indicated that adverse consequences of globalisation are disproportionately borne by women. Increased mechanization leading to displacement of female unskilled workers, increased migration of male workers in traditionally women-dominated areas, increase in female-headed household due to migration of males are some of the trends established in various studies.

Globalization has presented new challenges for the realization of the goal of women's equality, the gender impact of which has not been systematically evaluated fully. However, it is evident that there is a need for re-framing policies for access to employment and equality of employment. Benefits of the growing global economy have been unevenly distributed leading to wider economic disparities, the feminization of poverty, increased gender inequality through deteriorating working conditions and unsafe working environment especially in the informal economy and rural areas. Strategies need to be designed to enhance the capacity of women and empower them to meet the negative social and economic impacts, which may flow from the globalization process.

With upgradation of skills, opportunities for employment of women exist in several areas such as health services, food processing and crafts. Key areas of concern include women in small subsistence farming households, women workers in garment and textiles who will face increased competition after the phasing out of the Multi Fibre Agreement in 2005, and women displaced by new technologies in sectors such as construction, which have traditionally absorbed large numbers of women.

With the onset of trade liberalisation, women in India today are linked to the global economy to a very significant extent, as producers, entrepreneurs, service providers, consumers and citizens. There is a need to identify capacity constraints and entry barriers that prevent women from securing gains from trade. Trade- related awareness and capacity building of the women stakeholders need to be prioritised.

The globalization process has, in some countries, resulted in policy shifts in favour of more open trade and financial flows, privatization of state-owned enterprises and in many cases lower public spending particularly on social services. This change has transformed patterns of production and accelerated technological advances in information and communication and affected the lives of women, both as workers and consumers. In a large number of countries, particularly in developing and least developed countries, these changes have also adversely impacted on the lives of women and have increased inequality. The gender impact of these changes has not been systematically evaluated. Globalization has also affected cultural values, lifestyles and forms of communication.

In countries with economies in transition women are bearing most of the hardships induced by the economic restructuring and being the first to lose jobs in times of recession. They are being squeezed out from fast growth sectors. Loss of childcare facilities due to elimination or privatization of state work places, increased need for older care without the corresponding facilities, continuing inequality of access to training for finding re-employment and to productive assets for entering or expanding businesses are current challenges facing women in these countries.

12.2.3 Poor Implementation of Women-related Laws:
In a semi-industrialised country like India, the working class in destined to be one of the weaker sections of society. Moreover, society being male-dominated, female labour receives very poor recognition or value. Not that there are no statutory provisions. In fact, the Constitution of India provides equal

rights and opportunities to both the genders. In addition there are specific provisions for protection and welfare of working women in many of the labour laws. However, most of these statutes do not cover the units in small and informal sectors which are the predominant workplaces of women.

Even where they are covered by the statutes, the poor enforcement practically nullifies the provisions. Moreover, there is another tragic factor that has to be noted. The very laws which are meant for working women are paradoxically turned against their interests by unscrupulous employers.

If the employers find it difficult to bypass these provisions, they get rid of the women workers and thus strike at the economic base of their livelihood. All these factors need to be studied in depth while drafting policy and legal provisions for the working women in order to plug all possible loopholes.

For the reasons mentioned above, as also for the benefit of working women, their union leaders—and for all those who are interested in the welfare of women workers—knowledge of existing provisions of labour laws is very essential. Women's emancipation is part of India's general developmental plans but government action can be neither effective nor adequate unless women themselves become more aware of their rights and the corresponding responsibilities. Every woman is a working woman, whether she works in the home or outside it. Many women work to earn money. Working women must know that they have some basic rights which are given by the law.

Though India has created protective legislations for women, the enactments have not been easy to implement. The very vastness of the country, the scattered nature of women workers, their lack of education and legal literacy, indifferent attitude of bureaucracy and the general status of women in society have added to vulnerability of women. This is true not only of rural unorganised women, but to an extent of the urban women workers also.

Proactive measures that overcome barriers and facilitate

participation, such as hostels for women, scholarships, transport, training materials and loans, should be made available on a large scale. Women's vocational training programme should be expanded along with institutional network providing training facilities exclusively for women.

In order to promote skills and employability of women, the sectors which employ a large number of women need to be identified. These may include construction, home-based traditional crafts or piece rate work, financial and health services as well as agricultural sectors.

Gender stereotyping in vocational courses should be eliminated to encourage women participation in non-traditional occupations, including existing and emerging technological fields.

12.3 Skill Development for Unorganized (Informal) Sector Workers

As per the survey carried out by the National Sample Survey Organization in the year 2009-10, the total employment, in both organized and unorganized sectors in the country was of the order of 46.5 crore comprising of around 2.8 crore in the organized sector and the balance 43.7 crore workers in the unorganized sector. Out of 43.7 crore workers in the unorganized sector, there are 24.6 crore workers employed in agricultural sector, about 4.4 crore in construction work and remaining in manufacturing and service.

Thus, approximately 93 percent of India's workforce is in the unorganized sector. The sector cuts across all economic activities and includes rural and urban areas. It contributes to about 60 percent of the country's GDP. Strengthening the skill base of the unorganized sector will improve productivity, working conditions, labour rights, social security and living standards.

Separate institutional mechanism should be explored to plan, implement and monitor the skill development efforts for the unorganised sector which, inter alia, include weavers, handloom workers, fishermen and fisherwomen, toddy tappers, leather workers, plantation labour, beedi workers.

12.3.1 Meaning, Size and Characteristics of Unorganized Workers

The unorganised sector is equated with the unprotected segment of the labour market where entry is free, labour turnover is high, wages are significantly lower, and the workers, generally, lack legal protection. This sector includes the self-employed, home-based workers, workers in small and tiny industries, agricultural labour etc. The basic point that one has to remember here is that this sector is not homogenous.

The First National Commission on Labour (1969) stated that unorganised labour was a group of workers who cannot be identified by a definition but could be described as those who have not been able to organise in pursuit of a common objective because of constraints such as: (a) casual nature of employment, (b) ignorance and illiteracy, (c) small size of establishments with low capital investment per person employed, (d) scattered nature of establishments and (e) superior strength of the employer operating singly or in combination.

The size of the unorganised sector labour has been growing because of shrinkage of employment in the organised sector as well as authority.

Unorganised workers, in both self-employed and wage employed categories, remain, by and large, legally unrecognised as workers, which implies that the existing laws related to minimum wages or social security are not applied to them. Besides the lack of legal recognition, lack of a designated *business place* also works to increase their vulnerability and exposes them to exploitation by the authorities. Further, the dispersed nature of workplace makes organisation of these workers and enterprises more difficult, further adding to their invisibility.

According to the final report of the National Commission for Enterprises in the Unorganised Sector (NCEUS) [Chairman: Arjun Sengupta] released in April 2009, workers in the unorganized (or informal) sector constitute more than 93 percent of the total workforce of India. Unorganized sector workers are those who do not have any job security, income security or social security and are therefore extremely vulnerable to exogenous shocks.

The workers in the informal economy are clearly the overwhelming proportion of the workforce and most of these suffer from various forms of insecurities and vulnerabilities. It follows that policies have to focus on improving their conditions. However, the extent to which policy should focus upon increasing the share of the workforce in the organized sector has been a matter of some debate.

Broadly, unorganized workers have concentrated in a small number of activity groups. Among men, most of the wage workers are engaged either in some kind of manufacturing, construction, trading or transport activities. Among women, most of the informal workers are engaged in either some kind of manufacturing, construction activities or just domestic services.

Casual workers constitute about one-fifth of the workers in the unorganized non-agricultural sector. Among the casual workers, more than half are engaged in the construction sector, followed by one-fifth in the manufacturing sector.

12.3.2 Target Groups in the Unorganized Sector for Skill Development: The target groups in the unorganized sector include, among others, the following:
1. Own-account workers.
2. Workers and apprentices in micro enterprises.
3. Unpaid family workers.
4. Casual labourers.
5. Home-based workers.
6. Peripatetic workers.
7. Migrant labourers.
8. Out of school youth and adults in need of skills.
9. Farmers and artisans in rural areas.

In order to encourage participation in skill development, entry barriers such as educational qualification, transportation, loss of wages, problem of language etc. should be suitably addressed.

12.3.3 Training Providers:

1. Various institutions including schools and public/private training institutions/civil society organizations/NGOs etc. should be encouraged to conduct skill development programmes for the unorganised sector.
2. Mobile training vans should also be deployed in rural and remote areas where training infrastructure is awfully deficient.
3. Skill development centres should conduct skill development programmes primarily to support services and unorganised sector.
4. Public training institutions need to be given greater managerial and academic autonomy to design and offer programmes that meet the requirements of local economy and specific target groups.
5. Flexible delivery strategy and patterns that suit the needs of the target groups, such as part/full time and on/off site training, should be adopted.
6. Training should be predominantly short-term to encourage participation.
7. Arrangements should be made for the testing and certification of skills acquired in non-formal and informal arrangements.

Limited access to human and physical capital among workers acts as a major constraint on access to employment, quality of employment or growth of self-employment activities. A substantial proportion of wage workers in agriculture and non-agriculture are either landless or land poor. Self-employed in agriculture have better access to land ownership. In modern times, education is important to obtain gainful, productive and remunerative employment. Unorganized workers have the lowest level of education and literacy. Scheduled castes (SCs), scheduled tribes (STs) and Muslims are overwhelmingly concentrated in the unorganized sector and in self-employed activities to meet their livelihood needs.

13

Recent Initiatives for Skill Development

Skills and knowledge are the driving forces of economic growth and social development for any country. India currently faces a severe shortage of well-trained, skilled workers. It is estimated that only 2.3 percent of the workforce in India has undergone formal skill training as compared to 68 percent in the UK, 75 percent in Germany, 52 percent in USA, 80 percent in Japan and 96 percent in South Korea.

Large sections of the educated workforce have little or no job skills, making them largely unemployable. Therefore, India must focus on scaling up skill training efforts to meet the demands of employers and drive economic growth.

India's annual skilling capacity was estimated at approximately 7 million during the period 2013-2014. Apart from meeting its own demand, India has the potential to provide a skilled workforce to fill the expected shortfall in the ageing developed world. India is one of the youngest nations in the world, with more than 54 percent of the total population below 25 years of age and over 62 percent of the population in the working age group (15-59 years). The country's population pyramid is expected to bulge across the 15-59 age group over the next decade.

This demographic advantage is predicted to last only until 2040. India therefore has a very narrow timeframe to harness its demographic dividend and to overcome its skill shortages. The enormity of India's skilling challenge is further aggravated by the fact that skill training efforts cut across multiple sectors and require the involvement of diverse stakeholders such as: (a) multiple government departments at the centre and state levels, (b) private training providers, (c) educational and training institutions, (d) employers, (e) industry associations and (f) assessment and certification bodies and trainees. All these stakeholders need to align their work together in order to achieve the target of 'Skill India'.

13.1 National Policy for Skill Development and Entrepreneurship (NPSDE), 2015

The Ministry of Labour and Employment, Government of India, had formulated a National Policy on Skill Development in 2009. The objective of this policy was to empower all individuals through improved skills, knowledge, nationally and internationally recognized qualifications to gain access to decent employment and ensure India's competitiveness in the global market.

On July 15, 2015, Prime Minister Shri Narendra Modi launched the National Policy for Skill Development and Entrepreneurship (NPSDE), 2015 along with the following three other landmark initiatives of the Ministry of Skill Development and Entrepreneurship:
- National Skill Development Mission.
- Pradhan Mantri Kaushal Vikas Yojana (PMKVY).
- Skill Loan Scheme.

The 2009 policy was, thus, superseded by NPSDE, 2015. The new policy tries to bring the world of education and training closer to the world of work so as to enable them together build a strong India.

The Ministry of Skill Development and Entrepreneurship, Government of India, is an integral part of the government policy on *Sabka Saath, Sabka Vikaas* and its commitment to overall human resources development to take advantage of the demographic profile of India in the coming years. The objective of NPSDE, 2015 is to meet the challenge of skilling at scale with speed and standard (quality). It aims to provide an umbrella framework to all skilling activities being carried out within the country, and to align them to common standards and link the skilling with demand centres. In addition to laying down the objectives and expected outcomes, it also identifies the various institutional frameworks which can act as the vehicle to reach the expected outcomes. The national policy also provides clarity and coherence on how skill development efforts across the country can be aligned within the existing institutional arrangements. This policy links skills development to improved employability and productivity.

The salient features and provisions of NPSDE, 2015 are presented below.

13.1.1 Vision and Mission:

Vision: To create an ecosystem of empowerment by skilling on a large scale at speed with high standards and to promote a culture of innovation based entrepreneurship which can generate wealth and employment so as to ensure Sustainable livelihoods for all citizens in the country.

Mission: The mission is to:
- Create a demand for skilling across the country.
- Correct and align skilling with required competencies.
- Connect the supply of skilled human resources with sectoral demands.
- Certify and assess in alignment with global and national standards.
- Catalyse an ecosystem wherein productive and innovative entrepreneurship germinates, sustains and grows leading to creation of a more dynamic entrepreneurial economy and more formal wage employment.

13.1.2 Objectives of NPSDE, 2015: The core objective of NPSDE, 2015 is to empower the individuals by enabling them to realize their full potential through a process of lifelong learning where competencies are accumulated via instruments such as credible certifications, credit accumulation and transfer etc. As individuals grow, the society and nation also benefit from their productivity and growth. This will involve the following:

1. Make quality vocational training aspirational for both youth and employers whereby youth sees it as a matter of choice and employer acknowledges the productivity linked

to skilled workforce by paying the requisite premium.
2. Ensure both vertical and horizontal pathways to skilled workforce for further growth by providing seamless integration of skill training with formal education.
3. Focus on an outcome-based approach towards quality skilling that on the one hand results in increased employability and better livelihoods for individuals, and on the other hand translates into improved productivity across primary, secondary and tertiary sectors.
4. Increase the capacity and quality of training infrastructure and trainers to ensure equitable and easy access to every citizen.
5. Address human resources needs by aligning supply of skilled workers with sectoral requirements of industry and the country's strategic priorities including flagship programmes like 'Make in India'.
6. Establish an IT-based information system for aggregating demand and supply of skilled workforce which can help in matching and connecting supply with demand.
7. Promote national standards in the skilling space through active involvement of employers in setting occupational standards, helping develop curriculum, providing apprenticeship opportunities, participating in assessments, and providing gainful employment to skilled workforce with adequate compensation. Operationalize a well-defined quality assurance framework aligned with global standards to facilitate mobility of labour.
8. Leverage modern technology to ensure scale, access and outreach, in addition to ease of delivering content and monitoring results.
9. Recognise the value of on-the-job training, by making apprenticeships in actual work environments an integral part of all skill development efforts.
10. Ensure that the skilling needs of the socially and geographically disadvantaged and marginalized groups—like the scheduled castes (SCs), scheduled tribes (STs), other

backward classes (OBCs), minorities, differently-abled persons—are appropriately taken care of.
11. Promote increased participation of women in the workforce through appropriate skilling and gender mainstreaming of training.
12. Promote commitment and ownership of all stakeholders towards skill development and create an effective coordination mechanism.

The core objective of the entrepreneurship framework is to co-ordinate and strengthen factors essential for the growth of entrepreneurship across the country. This would include as under:
1. Promote entrepreneurship culture and make it aspirational.
2. Encourage entrepreneurship as a viable career option through advocacy.
3. Enhance support for potential entrepreneurs through mentorship and networks.
4. Integrate entrepreneurship education in the formal education system.
5. Foster innovation-driven and social entrepreneurship to address the needs of the population at the *bottom of the pyramid.*
6. Ensure ease of doing business by reducing entry and exit barriers.
7. Facilitate access to finance through credit and market linkages.
8. Promote entrepreneurship amongst women.
9. Broaden the base of entrepreneurial supply by meeting specific needs of both socially and geographically disadvantaged sections of the society including SCs, STs, OBCs, minorities, differently-abled persons.

13.1.3 Policy Framework for Skill Development: Eleven-point Strategy: The policy framework has been developed to accomplish the vision of 'Skill India' by adhering to the objectives mentioned above. The framework outlines the following 11 major paradigms and enablers to achieve these

objectives of skilling India:
1. Aspiration and advocacy.
2. Capacity.
3. Quality.
4. Synergy.
5. Mobilization and engagement.
6. Global partnerships.
7. Outreach.
8. ICT enablement.
9. Trainers and assessors.
10. Inclusivity.
11. Promotion of skilling among women.

13.1.4 Policy Framework for Entrepreneurship: Nine-point Strategy: The entrepreneurship policy framework has been developed to address the objectives. Vibrant entrepreneurship requires support from an enabling ecosystem of culture, finance, expertise, infrastructure, skills and business-friendly regulations. Many government and non-government organizations are playing enabling roles across each of these crucial supporting elements. This policy framework, cognizant of the need for the full ecosystem to be present to unlock entrepreneurial potential, proposes the following nine part entrepreneurship strategy:

1. Educate and equip potential and early stage entrepreneurs across India.
2. Connect entrepreneurs to peers, mentors and incubators.
3. Support entrepreneurs through entrepreneurship hubs (e-hubs).
4. Catalyse a culture shift to encourage entrepreneurship.
5. Encourage entrepreneurship among under-represented groups.
6. Promote entrepreneurship amongst women.
7. Improve ease of doing business.
8. Improve access to finance.
9. Foster social entrepreneurship and grassroots innovations.

13.1.5 Governance Structure and Financing:
A. Governance Structure: Ministry of Skill Development

and Entrepreneurship has been created to fulfil the vision of a 'Skilled India' where human resources development is the primary focus. MSDE will be responsible for co-ordination with all concerned for evolving an appropriate skill development framework, removal of disconnect between demand for, and supply of, skilled manpower, skill upgradation, building of new skills, innovative thinking and talents for existing and future jobs. MSDE will also play the lead role in ensuring the implementation of the National Policy for Skill Development and Entrepreneurship, 2015.

Skill development and entrepreneurship are complementary to each other. The key stakeholders include Central Ministries/Departments, State Governments, and industry/employers. There is a need to ensure alignment of the efforts of all stakeholders in skill and entrepreneurship landscape towards a common goal. While MSDE will co-ordinate and converge all efforts in this space, the relevant Central Ministries/Departments, State Governments and industry/employers are expected to fulfil the roles and responsibilities pertaining to their domain as laid down in the National Policy for Skill Development and Entrepreneurship.

The objectives and targets under the National Policy will be met in mission mode approach. The National Skill Development Mission will be launched to implement and co-ordinate all skilling efforts in the country towards the objectives laid down in the policy. The Mission will be housed in MSDE and the key institutional mechanisms for achieving the objectives of the Mission will be divided into a three-tier structure at the Centre to steer, drive and execute the Mission's objectives. The Mission will consist of a governing council at apex level, a steering committee and a mission directorate (along with an Executive Committee) as the executive arm of the Mission. At State level, States will be encouraged to create State Skill Development Missions (SSDM) along the lines of National Skill Development Mission with a steering committee and mission directorate at State level. States will, in turn, be supported by district committees at the functional tier.

Mission directorate will be supported by three other institutions: National Skill Development Agency (NSDA), National Skill Development Corporation (NSDC), and Directorate General of Training (DGT) all of which will have horizontal/vertical linkages with Mission Directorate to facilitate smooth functioning of the national institutional mechanism.

B. Financing: Public funds (funding by Central Government, State Governments and grant-based schemes) are finite and will not be able to cover the magnitude of the challenge of Skilling India. Hence, alternative sources of funds are required. Therefore, all stakeholders, the Government, both at Centre and States, public and private enterprises, and the direct beneficiary (the individual), would contribute in mobilizing financial or in-kind resources for skill development. The success of the policy will depend upon the quantum of resources mobilised from all stakeholders.

National Skill Development Fund (NSDF) has been set up by Government of India with the objective of encouraging skill development in the country. A public trust set up by Government of India is the custodian of the Fund. The Fund acts as a receptacle for all donations, contribution in cash or kind from all contributors (including Government, multilateral organizations, corporations etc.) for furtherance of the objectives of the Fund.

To channelize the interest of a plethora of organisations to participate in the mission of Skill India, a strategic vehicle to create a multiplier effect on skilling has been devised. A 'Resource Optimization for Skilling at Scale Platform' has been proposed by the Government to act as a demand-responsive and flexible vehicle to tackle the issues of skills shortages through skill development, job creation and placement at scale. It will serve as the aggregator vehicle for pooling the funds of multilateral agencies, companies, foundations, NGOs and individuals for skilling interventions by leveraging existing infrastructure and resources. The platform will also be subjected to timely audits to ensure that the contributions are used for the intended purpose.

To attract funds from industry, companies will be encouraged to spend at least 25 percent of their corporate social responsibility (CSR) funds on skill development initiatives directly or through NSDF. Further, industry should earmark at least 2 percent of its payroll bill (including for contract labour) for skill development initiatives in their respective sectors. These funds can be channelized for skill development activities either through respective SSCs or through NSDF.

All Government schemes across sectors will be encouraged to apportion a certain percentage (10 percent) of the scheme budget towards skilling of human resources in local regions in the required sector. These funds could be used for implementation directly or be routed through NSDF. Government may consider other options including cess etc. to raise funds for meeting the requirements of this sector.

End-user funding through a basic fee paying model will also be a key medium for funding training activities. However, the Government believes that the inability to pay training costs should not stop any desirous citizen in the country from acquiring any certified skill training. The Government will promote grant of scholarships, rewards and skill vouchers (SV) for funding of training costs. It will also be ensured that for all government schemes, direct benefit transfer (DBT) will be used as a mechanism for payment disbursement.

A Credit Guarantee Fund for skill development and a National Credit Guarantee Trustee Company (NCGTC) has been set up to support the initiative of loans for the purpose of skilling and will be used to leverage credit financing in the skill landscape. It will be further expanded to ensure greater outreach and access to all citizens. Similarly, a Credit Guarantee Fund for Entrepreneurship Development worth ₹ 3,000 crore per year has already been initiated under Prime Minister MUDRA Yojana through NCGTC.

13.1.6 Monitoring and Evaluation: The National Policy for Skill Development and Entrepreneurship has been structured as an outcome-oriented policy. It is, therefore, desirable that there should be regular monitoring and evaluation of the initiatives to ensure that best practices can be scaled and corrective measures can be introduced. The main idea of having a robust monitoring and evaluation mechanism is to ensure successful implementation of the policy initiatives.

Government desires to set up a policy implementation unit (PIU) so as to review the implementation and progress of the various initiatives under this policy. The PIU will be housed in MSDE with Secretary as the Chairperson and representation from NITI Aayog. For the smooth functioning of the PIU, it will also ensure constant consultation with stakeholders to get feedback so as to enable improvements, if required.

The PIU will perform the following functions:
1. List all the action points as mentioned in the policy on which further action is required.
2. Identify all the agencies involved and map the actionable points to the responsible agency.
3. Co-ordinate with all the agencies involved and help them devise a draft outline as well as timelines for the implementation of the initiatives assigned to them.
4. Timelines that are explicitly mentioned in the policy for certain initiatives will supersede other timelines.
5. Act as a co-ordinating body for all the implementing agencies and support them to enhance their efficiency.
6. PIU will also conduct monthly review of the action points and nudge them if the progress is not as expected.

PIU will be made responsible to the NSDM. It will present its reports, findings and the way forward to the Steering Committee of the Mission every quarter. PIU will be the main body overlooking the implementation of policy.

13.1.7 Impact Assessment: For the purpose of undertaking impact assessment, annual as well as 5 year target will be set for each stakeholder by the PIU. Impact assessment

will be undertaken to ensure that the targets are met well within the time frame. The stakeholders will also be subject to a quarterly review. For the purpose of impact assessment, the following monitoring indicators, amongst others, are prescribed:
1. Number/registrations of youth interested in skilling.
2. Number of youth registered in training programmes.
3. Number of youth assessed and certified by regulatory authorities.
4. Placement rate of skilled trainees.
5. Number of accredited/affiliated training providers/centres.
6. Number of certified trainers, sector-wise.
7. Number of certified assessors, sector-wise.
8. Number of job roles for which QPs and NOS have been developed.
9. Existing public infrastructure leveraged for training.
10. Number of skilled persons engaged in overseas employment.
11. Reduction in sectoral demand and supply gap.
12. Amount of private funds mobilised for encouraging skill development and entrepreneurship.
13. Percentage of socially and geographically disadvantaged groups enrolled in training programmes.
14. Percentage of skilled youth that are self-employed.
15. Infrastructure dedicated for entrepreneurship support.
16. Number of schools running skills and entrepreneurship courses.
17. Percentage of socially and geographically disadvantaged groups engaged in self employment.

With the help of the PIU, it will be easier to monitor the implementation of the policy initiatives and take corrective measures in case of non-compliance. A mid-term review of the policy will be undertaken based on impact assessment by a third party. The policy can be considered for review after 5 years, based on learnings from implementation of the policy.

In short, NPSDE, 2015 has four thrust areas. It addresses

key obstacles to skilling, including low aspirational value, lack of integration with formal education, lack of focus on outcomes, low quality of training infrastructure and trainers etc. Further, it seeks to align supply and demand for skills by bridging existing skill gaps, promoting industry engagement, operationalising a quality assurance framework, leverage technology and promoting greater opportunities for apprenticeship training.

Equity is also a focus of NPSDE, 2015, which targets skilling opportunities for socially/geographically marginalised and disadvantaged groups. Skill development and entrepreneurship programmes for women are a specific focus area. In the entrepreneurship domain, it seeks to educate and equip potential entrepreneurs, both within and outside the formal education system. It also seeks to connect entrepreneurs to mentors, incubators and credit markets, foster innovation and entrepreneurial culture, improve ease of doing business and promote a focus on social entrepreneurship.

The primary objective of NPSDE, 2015 is to meet the challenge of skilling at scale with speed, standard (quality) and sustainability. It aims to provide an umbrella framework to all skilling activities being carried out within the country, to align them to common standards and link skilling with demand centres. In addition to laying down the objectives and expected outcomes, it also identifies the overall institutional framework which will act as a vehicle to reach the expected outcomes. Skills development is the shared responsibility of the key stakeholders, viz. Government, the entire spectrum of corporate sector, community-based organizations, highly qualified and dedicated individuals, industry and trade organisations and other stakeholders.

NPSDE, 2015 links skill development to improved employability and productivity, paving the way forward for inclusive growth in the country. The skill strategy is complemented by specific efforts to promote entrepreneurship in order to create ample opportunities for the skilled workforce.

13.2 National Skill Development Mission (NSDM)

13.2.1 Launching of Skill India Mission: National Skill Development Mission (NSDM) was approved by the Union Cabinet on July 1, 2015, and officially launched by the Prime Minister on July 15, 2015 on the occasion of World Youth Skills Day. 18,000 plus ITI graduating students received job offer letters on the occasion of World Youth Skills Day. Government has set a target to provide skill training to 40.02 crore people by 2022.

NSDM has been developed to create convergence across sectors and States in terms of skill training activities. Further, to achieve the vision of Skilled India, NSDM would not only consolidate and co-ordinate skilling efforts, but also expedite decision making across sectors to achieve skilling at scale with speed and standards. It will be implemented through a streamlined institutional mechanism driven by Ministry of Skill Development and Entrepreneurship (MSDE).

The Ministry of Skill Development and Entrepreneurship (earlier Department of Skill Development and Entrepreneurship, first created in July 2014) was set up in November 2014 to drive the Skill India agenda in a Mission Mode in order to converge existing skill training initiatives and combine scale and quality of skilling efforts, with speed.

The Ministry, therefore, launched NSDM which will provide the overall institutional framework to rapidly implement and scale up skill development efforts across India. It seeks to provide the institutional capacity to train a minimum of 300 million skilled people by the year 2022.

13.2.2 Objectives of NSDM: NSDM seeks to:
1. Create an end-to-end implementation framework for skill development, which provides opportunities for life-long learning. This includes incorporation of skilling in the school curriculum, providing opportunities for quality long and short-term skill training, by providing gainful employment and ensuring career progression that meets the aspirations of trainees.

2. Align employer/industry demand and workforce productivity with trainees' aspirations for sustainable livelihoods, by creating a framework for outcome focused training.
3. Establish and enforce cross-sectoral, nationally and internationally acceptable standards for skill training in the country by creating a sound quality assurance framework for skilling, applicable to all Ministries, States and private training providers.
4. Build capacity for skill development in critical unorganized sectors (such as the construction sector, where there are few opportunities for skill training) and provide pathways for re-skilling and up-skilling workers in these identified sectors, to enable them to transition into formal sector employment.
5. Ensure sufficient, high quality options for long-term skilling, benchmarked to internationally acceptable qualification standards, which will ultimately contribute to the creation of a highly skilled workforce.
6. Develop a network of quality instructors/trainers in the skill development ecosystem by establishing high quality teacher training institutions.
7. Leverage existing public infrastructure and industry facilities for scaling up skill training and capacity building efforts.
8. Offer a passage for overseas employment through specific programmes mapped to global job requirements and benchmarked to international standards.
9. Enable pathways for transitioning between the vocational training system and the formal education system, through a credit transfer system.
10. Promote convergence and co-ordination between skill development efforts of all Central Ministries and Departments/States/implementing agencies.
11. Support weaker and disadvantaged sections of society through focused outreach programmes and targeted skill development activities.

12. Propagate aspirational value of skilling among youth, by creating social awareness on value of skill training.
13. Maintain a national database, known as the labour market information system (LMIS), which will act as a portal for matching the demand and supply of skilled workforce in the country. The LMIS, will on the one hand provide citizens with vital information on skilling initiatives across the country. On the other, it will also serve as a platform for monitoring the performance of existing skill development programmes, running in every Indian state.

13.2.3 Institutional Mechanisms: Key institutional mechanisms for achieving the objectives of NSDM have been divided into three tiers. NSDM will consist of a governing council at the apex level, a steering committee, and a mission directorate as the executive arm of the Mission.

Mission Directorate will be supported by three other institutions: National Skill Development Agency (NSDA), National Skill Development Corporation (NSDC), and Directorate General of Training (DGT)—all of which will have linkages with Mission Directorate to facilitate smooth functioning of the national institutional mechanism. These three agencies would continue to lie under the umbrella of Ministry of Skill Development and Entrepreneurship.

At the State level, States will be encouraged to create State Skill Development Missions (SSDMs) along the lines of National Skill Development Mission with a Steering Committee and Mission Directorate at State level. States will, in turn, be supported by District Committees at the functional tier.

13.2.4 NSDM Strategy: Seven sub-missions have been proposed initially to act as building blocks for achieving overall objectives of NSDM. They are:
1. Institutional training.
2. Infrastructure.
3. Convergence.
4. Trainers.
5. Overseas employment.

6. Sustainable livelihoods.
7. Leveraging public infrastructure.

The sub-missions can be added to/amended as per decision of Governing Council. The power to identify sub-missions in crucial areas which require immediate attention will lie with governing council chaired by the Prime Minister. Executive guidelines and detailing of each sub-mission will be done by executive committee headed by secretary, MSDE.

Key focus areas of the sub-missions include: (a) addressing the long-term and short-term skilling needs through revamp of existing institutional training framework and establishing new institutions, (b) undertaking sector-specific skill training initiatives, (c) ensuring convergence of existing skill development programmes, (d) leveraging existing public infrastructure for skilling, (e) focusing on training of trainers, (f) facilitating overseas employment, and (g) promoting sustainable livelihoods.

Sub-Missions have currently been proposed in priority areas. The number of sub-missions can be modified as per changing skill requirements and challenges. Each sub-mission will be headed by a Joint Secretary or Director level officer designated as CEO, sourced from the public or private sector, who has a solid track record of implementing projects and achieving targets in a timely manner. The Sub-Mission's support team will consist of high performing individuals drawn from the public and private domains.

13.3 Pradhan Mantri Kaushal Vikas Yojana (PMKVY)

On July 15, 2015, Prime Minister Shri Narendra Modi launched the Pradhan Mantri Kaushal Vikas Yojana (PMKVY), 2015.

The slogan *Kaushal Bharat, Kushal Bharat* suggests that skilling Indians (*Kaushal Bharat*) will result in a happy, healthy, prosperous and strong nation (*Kushal Bharat*).

PMKVY is the flagship, demand-driven, reward-based skill training scheme of the Ministry of Skill Development and Entrepreneurship (MSDE). It is intended to incentivise skill training by providing financial rewards to candidates who successfully complete approved skill training programmes. For the first time, the skills of young people who lack formal certification, such as workers in India's vast unorganised sector, will be recognised. Through an initiative known as recognition of prior learning (RPL), 10 lakh youth will be assessed and certified for the skills that they already possess.

Under PMKVY, skill cards and skill certificates are awarded which allow trainees to share their skill identity with employers. Each skill card and skill certificate features a quick response code (QR Code), which can be read through a QR reader on mobile devices. Trainees can use these to share their skill qualifications with employers in a quick and reliable way during the job search process.

Approved for another four years (2016-2020) to benefit 10 million youth, training and assessment fees under PMKVY are completely paid by the Government.

13.3.1 Key Components of the Scheme: These are as under:

A. Short-term Training: Short-term training imparted at PMKVY training centres (TCs) is expected to benefit candidates of Indian nationality who are either school/college dropouts or unemployed. Apart from providing training according to the National Skills Qualification Framework (NSQF), TCs shall also impart training in soft skills, entrepreneurship, financial and digital literacy. Duration of the training varies per job role, ranging between 150 and 300 hours. Upon successful completion of their assessment, candidates shall be provided placement assistance by training partners (TPs). Under PMKVY, the entire training and assessment fees are paid by the Government. Payouts shall be provided to the TPs in alignment with the common norms. Trainings imparted under the short-term training component of the scheme shall be NSQF Level 5 and below.

B. Recognition of Prior Learning: Individuals with prior learning experience or skills shall be assessed and certified under the recognition of prior learning (RPL) component of the scheme. RPL aims to align the competencies of the unregulated workforce of the country to the NSQF. Project implementing agencies (PIAs), such as sector skill councils (SSCs) or any other agencies designated by MSDE/NSDC, shall be incentivized to implement RPL projects in any of the three project types (RPL Camps, RPL at Employers Premises and RPL Centres). To address knowledge gaps, PIAs may offer bridge courses to RPL candidates.

13.3.2 Special Projects: The special projects component of PMKVY envisages the creation of a platform that will facilitate trainings in special areas and/or premises of Government bodies, corporates or industry bodies, and trainings in special job roles not defined under the available qualification packs (QPs)/national occupational standards (NOSs). Special projects are projects that require some deviation from the terms and conditions of short-term training under PMKVY for any stakeholder. A proposing stakeholder can be either Government institutions of Central and State Government(s)/autonomous body/statutory body or any other equivalent body or corporates who desire to provide training to candidates.

13.3.3 Kaushal and Rozgar Mela: Social and community mobilisation is extremely critical for the success of PMKVY. Active participation of the community ensures transparency and accountability, and helps in leveraging the cumulative knowledge of the community for better functioning. In line with this, PMKVY assigns special importance to the involvement of the target beneficiaries through a defined mobilisation process. TPs shall conduct *Kaushal and Rozgar Melas* every 6 months with press/media coverage. They are also required to participate actively in national career service melas and on-ground activities.

13.3.4 Placement Guidelines: PMKVY envisages to link the aptitude, aspiration, and knowledge of the skilled workforce it creates with employment opportunities and demands in the market. Every effort thereby needs to be made by the PMKVY TCs to provide placement opportunities to candidates, trained and certified under the Scheme. TPs shall also provide support to entrepreneurship development.

13.3.5 Monitoring Guidelines: To ensure that high standards of quality are maintained by TCs, NSDC and empaneled inspection agencies shall use various methodologies, such as self-audit reporting, call validations, surprise visits, and monitoring through the skills development management system (SDMS). These methodologies shall be enhanced with the engagement of latest technologies.

The scheme will be implemented through the National Skill Development Corporation (NSDC).

13.4 Udaan

Udaan is a Special Industry Initiative for Jammu and Kashmir (J&K) in the nature of partnership between the corporates of India and Ministry of Home Affairs and implemented by National Skill Development Corporation. The programme aims to provide skills training and enhance the employability of unemployed youth of J&K. The scheme covers graduates, post-graduates and three year engineering diploma holders. It has two objectives:

- To provide an exposure to the unemployed graduates to the best of corporate India;
- To provide corporate India, an exposure to the rich talent pool available in the State.

The key stakeholders are:
- Ministry of Home Affairs (MHA): Chief Benefactors.
- State Government (Jammu and Kashmir).
- Corporates: Training Partners.
- Implementation Agency: NSDC.

The scheme aims to cover 40,000 youth of J&K over a period of 5 years and a sum of ₹ 750 crore has been earmarked for implementation of the scheme over a period of 5 years to cover other incidental expenses such as travel cost, boarding and lodging, stipend and travel and medical insurance cost for the trainees and administration cost. Further corporates are eligible for partial reimbursement of training expense incurred for the candidates who have been offered jobs.

13.5 Skill Loan Scheme

Launched on July 15, 2015, the scheme will make available loans ranging from ₹ 5,000-₹ 1.5 lakh to 34 lakh youth of India seeking to attend skill development programmes over the next 5 years.

References/Bibliography

References/Bibliography

Arnold, V.D. and T.D. Roach (1989), "Teaching: A Non-verbal Communication Event", *Business Education Forum,* 44, 18-20.

Ashwathappa, K. (1997), "Human Resource and Personnel Management", New Delhi: Tata- McGraw Hill.

Basu, C.R. (1987), "Human Resource Development", *Indian Journal of Commerce,* Vol X1, January-June, pp. 150-151.

Bohlander, George W. (2004), "Managing Human resources", OH: Thomson/South Western.

Byars, Lloyd L. (2000), "Human Resource Management", MA: Irwin/McGraw Hill.

Dayal, Ishwar (1989), "HRD in Indian Organizations: Current Perspectives and Future Issues", *Vikalpa,* Vol. 14, October-December.

Delors, J. (1996), "Learning: The Treasure Within", Report of UNESCO of the International Commission on Education for Twenty-first Century, UNESCO Publication, France.

Dreze, J. and A. Sen (1996), "India: Economic Development and Social Opportunity", New Delhi: Oxford University Press.

Drucker, P. (1974), "New Templates for Today's Organizations", *Harvard Business Review,* Vol. 52, pp. 1-45.

Fluitman, F. (2009), "Skills Development for the Informal Economy: Issues and Options in Vocational Education and Training in the Southern Partner Countries of the European Neighbourhood Policy", HTSP Limited.

Government of India, Ministry of Human Resources Development, "National Policy on Education, 1986".

——Ministry of Human Resources Development, "Report of Ramamutri Review Committee, 1990".

——Ministry of Human Resources Development, "Programme of Action on National Policy on Education (1986)", 1992.

——Ministry of Human Resources Development, "Report of the Steering Committee on Elementary and Adult Education for the Tenth Five year Plan (2002-2007)", 2001.

——Ministry of Human Resources Development, "Quality Education in a Global Era: Challenges to Equity and Opportunities for Diversity", Country Paper, 2000.

——Ministry of Human Resources Development, "Towards an Enlightened and Humane Society: NPE, 1986, A Review".

Hersey, Paul (1988), "Management of Organizational Behaviour", NJ: Prentice Hall.

Harrison, Rosemary and Kessels Joseph (1996), "Human Resource Development: Key Organizational Process in a Knowledge Economy", *Industrial Training*, Vol. 20/9, pp. 29-34.

Jackson, Susan E. and Randall S. Schuler (1990), "Challenges for Industrial/Organizational Psychologists", *American Psychologist*, February, Vol. 45, No. 2.

Kaur, Jaideep and Vikas Kuman (n.d.), "Competency Mapping: A Gap Analysis", *International Journal of Human Resource Management and Research*, Vol. 2, Issue 1.

Mathis, Robert L. and Jackson, John H. (1997), "Human Resource Management", MN: West Publishers.

Mondy, R. Wayne (193), "Human Resource Management", MA: Allyn and Bacon.

Mundle, S. (ed.) (1998), "Financing Human Resource Development in the Advanced Asian Economies", *World Development,* 26(4), April.

Pareek, U. and T.V. Rao (1982), "Designing and Managing Human Resources Systems", New Delhi.

Pillai, Radhakrishnan (2010), "Corporate Chanakya: Successful Management the Chanakaya Ways", New Delhi: Jaico Publishing House.

Singh, A.K. and A.K. Sen (1992), "HRD Culture: A Model", *MOI Management Journal*, Vol. 5, January, p. 113.

Wendy EA Ruona, Susan A lynham, Thomas J Chermack, Advances in Developing human resources, San Francisco : Aug 2003, vol 5

World Bank (2007), "Cultivating Knowledge and Skills to Grow African Agriculture", Washington D.C.

World Bank, L. Fox and M.S. Gaal (2008), "Working Out of Poverty", The World Bank, Washington D.C.

Yuvraj, R. (2011), "Competency Mapping", *International Journal of Scientific and Engineering Research*, Vol. 2, Issue 8, August.

Websites

Ministry of Skill Development and Entrepreneurship (MSDE)
Ministry of Human Resources Development

References/Bibliography

Ministry of Labour and Employment
Ministry of Micro, Small and Medium Enterprises (MoMSMEs)
Ministry of Social Justice and Empowerment
Ministry of Tribal Affairs
Ministry of Minority Affairs
Ministry of Women and Child Development (MWCD)
University Grants Commission (UGC)

Index

Index

A
Albert Bandura, 52
Andrew Brown, 87
Arjun Sengupta, 139
Asian Development bank
 (ADB), 33, 123
Attribution Theory, 54

B
Behaviourally-anchored
 Ranking Scale (BARS),
 62
Business Games, 80

C
Chanakya's Contribution
 to HRM, 4
Child Sex Ratio, 98
Classification of
 Competencies, 57
Cognitivism Theory, 53
Companies Act, 2013, 118
Compensation
 Management, 64
Competency Mapping, 57
Competing Value Model, 27
Core Competencies, 57
Corporate Social
 Responsibility (CSR),
 118

D
David J. Skyrme, 33

Degree of Urbanisation,
 102
Demographic Dividend
 Hypothesis, 104
Density of Population, 103
Department for International
 Development (DFID),
 123
Distributed Learning, 48
Double Burden of Work,
 131

E
Edwin B. Flippo, 75
Eleventh Five Year Plan
 (2007-12), 129
Employees Socialization, 66
Explicit Knowledge, 35

F
First National Commission
 on Labour (1969), 139
Functional/Professional
 Competencies, 57

G
Gap Analysis, 3
Gestalt Psychology, 53
Globalization and HRD, 6
Goals of HRD, 16

H
Human Capital, 9

Human Relations
  Movement, 16

I
Iceberg Model of
  Competency, 60
Indian Penal Code, 99
Internal Process Approach,
  26
Ivan Pavlov's Dog Theory,
  51

J
Job Analysis, 31
Job Rotation, 82

K
Kaushal and Rozgar Mela,
  159
Kautilya, 4
Knowledge Audit, 43
Knowledge Café, 42
Knowledge Harvesting, 43
Knowledge Management
  Barriers, 38
Knowledge Management
  Process, 37

L
L.M. Kendall, 62
Labour Market
  Information System
  (LMIS), 123
Learning Curve, 49
Life Expectancy, 100
Literacy Rate, 101

M
Maggie Haines, 33
Medical Termination of
  Pregnancies Act, 1971,
  99
Michael Armstrong, 75
Ministry of Corporate
  Affairs, 118
Ministry of Human
  Resource Development
  (MHRD), 110
Ministry of Labour and
  Employment, 111
Ministry of Skill
  Development and
  Entrepreneurship (MSDE),
  112
Most Favoured Nation
  (MFN) Rule, 11
Multi Fibre Agreement, 135
Multiple Sense Learning,
  48

N
National Commission for
  Enterprises in the
  Unorganized Sector
  (NCEUS), 139
National Credit Guarantee
  Trustee Company
  (NCGTC), 150
National Institute of
  Personnel Management
  of India, 1
National Policy for Skill
  Development and

Entrepreneurship (NPSDE), 2015, 143
National Skill Development Agency (NSDA), 122
National Skill Development Corporation (NSDC), 114
National Skill Development Fund (NSDF), 120
National Skill Development Mission (NSDM), 154

O
Organizational Analysis, 77
Organizational Characteristics, 92
Organizational Health, 93
Organizational Socialization, 66
Overall Sex Ratio, 97

P
P.C. Smith, 62
Persons with Disabilities Act, 1995, 129
Peter Drucker, 33
Philips C. Grant, 31
Population Policy of 2000, 100
Pradhan Mantri Kaushal Vikas Yojana (PMKVY), 157
Pre-conception and Pre-natal Diagnostic Techniques (Prohibition of Misuse) Act, 99
Prime Minister MUDRA Yojna, 150

R
R.P. Billimoria, 71

S
Sabka Saath, Sabka Vikaas, 143
SECI Model of Knowledge Dimensions, 36
Skills Innovation Initiative, 124
Skill Loan Scheme, 161
Social Function Model, 30
Social Learning Theory, 52
State Skill Development Missions (SSDMs), 107
Steer's Multi-dimensional Perspective, 28
System Resource Approach, 26

T
Tacit Knowledge, 35
Theories of Learning, 50
Time Dimensional Model, 29
Total Quality Management (TQM), 11
Training, Education and

Development, 17
Types of Knowledge, 35
Types of Organizational Cultures, 89

U
Udaan, 160

V
Vishnugupta, 4

W
Whole vs. Part Learning, 47
Work-life Balance, 2
World Trade Organization (WTO), 10